The FLUME GORGE AT FRANCONIA NOTCH

The FLUME GORGE AT FRANCONIA NOTCH

MICHAEL J. MADDIGAN

THE History PRESS

Published by The History Press
Charleston, SC
www.historypress.com

Front cover, top: J.V. Hartman & Co. *In the Flume, Franconia Notch, White Mountains, N.H.*, lithographic postcard, circa 1920. *Author's collection*.
Front cover, bottom: Kilburn Brothers. *Flume below the Boulder*, albumen silver print stereograph, circa 1875. *Courtesy of the Boston Public Library*.
Back cover, top: *The Flume, Franconia Notch, N.H.*, souvenir decal, circa 1950. *Author's collection.*
Back cover, bottom: Detroit Publishing Company. *Looking Down the Flume*, glass negative, circa 1910. *Courtesy of the Library of Congress.*

First published 2019

Manufactured in the United States

ISBN 9781467142687

Library of Congress Control Number: 2019932641

I long sometimes to have mountains, ravines, and flumes like that in Lincoln, New Hampshire, within reach of my eyes and feet.

—Ralph Waldo Emerson, 1843

CONTENTS

ACKNOWLEDGEMENTS

The author wishes to gratefully acknowledge the assistance of Carol Riley, president of the Upper Pemigewasset Historical Society and director of the Lincoln Public Library; Bill Ross and the staff of the Milne Special Collections, Dimond Library, University of New Hampshire; the staffs of the Grafton County Registry of Deeds and the New Hampshire State Library; Becky Fullerton, archivist, Appalachian Mountain Club; Jacob M. Scheff, registrar, Indiana State Museum and Historic Sites; the New York Public Library; the Boston Public Library; the Library of Congress; and the J. Paul Getty Museum, Los Angeles. All were generous with their assistance, and this work would not have been possible without them. Additional thanks go to Mike Kinsella and the team at The History Press both for their support with this and previous projects as well as for the phenomenal work they do popularizing local history.

INTRODUCTION

Deep in New Hampshire's White Mountains low on a flank of Mount Liberty near Franconia Notch lies the Flume, a granite-walled cleft named for its resemblance to the raceway of a water-powered mill. Once European Americans became aware of it in the first decades of the nineteenth century, the chasm began to attract the curious, eager to view "what nature looks like in our dreams."[1] Since that time, the Flume has become an iconic New Hampshire landmark with an important place in the state's recreational history. This book is an exploration of that history that examines the tourist experience at the Flume over the past two hundred years and touches upon efforts to balance recreational development with wilderness conservation at the site.

One of the earliest tourist descriptions of the Flume was recorded in the journal of future historian Francis Parkman, who visited on July 30, 1841:

> *This Flume is a huge natural trough of rock through which runs, in a succession of falls and rapids,* [Flume Brook,] *a branch of the river Pemigewasset. On each side of the stream high cliffs rise perpendicularly and run for many rods facing each other. Their black sides are smooth, and continually dropping moisture, for the forest above extends its branches from the edges so that the light of the sun can scarcely penetrate the ravine. Standing on the rocks at the bottom and looking up, you see huge decayed trunks and branches extending across the narrow strip of sky visible between the edges of the cliffs, and the edges themselves are overgrown with*

N.W. Pease. *The Flume from Below, Looking Up*, albumen silver print stereograph, circa 1865. *Courtesy of the Miriam and Ira D. Wallach Division of Art, Print and Photographs: Photography Collection, New York Public Library.*

> *masses of wet and green moss which hang dripping from them. Knotted and distorted pines, rooted in the crevices, fling their boughs across; and even those, though living, are covered with damp mosses....Beneath this, the stream foams down over a bed of rocks and rushes forward among the stones and accumulated trunks of trees which intercept its course.*[2]

Early nineteenth-century visitors drawn largely from New England's educated and literate classes called the Flume "sublime." In the rush to observe its wonders, intellectuals, artists, poets, scientists and politicians began flocking to Franconia Notch in the late 1830s to see it, minds reeling and mouths agape as they contemplated their place in the world and their relationship to God beside it.

The following decade, these contemplative recreationalists who regarded the Flume as a place for moral and spiritual renewal gave way to an influx of tourists who came for a more social experience, their presence facilitated by the arrival of the railroad at the edge of the mountains in 1850. Further fostering the Flume's development as a locus of social tourism was the Flume House hotel, which, owned in common with the Flume, encouraged visitation and established the foundation for the commercialization of Franconia Notch. By 1860, the Flume had become a required stop on nearly every New Hampshire tourist's itinerary, and it has remained so ever since.

Isaac Sprague. *The Flume Near Lincoln*, in William Oakes, *Scenery of the White Mountains*, 1848. *Author's collection.*

Though the Flume weathered late nineteenth-century industrial threats in the form of railroads and extensive lumbering, which imperiled the nature-seeking experience of Franconia Notch's visitors, increasing commodification of the Flume in the early twentieth century brought with it new dangers. In the 1920s, the Flume's proprietors who regarded the chasm as a fiscal rather than natural resource sought to wring as much revenue as possible from it, igniting an ongoing debate concerning the commercialization of New Hampshire's natural attractions.

Between 1928 and 1947, the Flume's new owner, the Society for the Protection of New Hampshire Forests, looked to restrict commercialization. While promoting greater accessibility, enhancing safety and furthering visitor enjoyment by cutting new paths and featuring "newly discovered" attractions, these efforts remained secondary to the society's mission of forest conservation. Since 1947, the Flume has been maintained as part of Franconia Notch State Park by the State of New Hampshire, which has sought to balance recreation with preservation. Under the state's stewardship, the Flume has changed little; it continues to offer an experience virtually unaltered from that of the 1930s, allowing visitors to enjoy the site as their grandparents once did. However, the continuing

Detroit Publishing Company. *Looking Down the Flume*, glass negative, circa 1910. *Courtesy of the Library of Congress.*

popularity of the Flume brings with it the challenge of potential overuse and growing ecological pressures.

For those of us raised in New England, a summer trip to Franconia Notch with a visit to the Flume was obligatory, a rite of passage and a source of long-standing memories. Three and a half decades after he visited as a child in June 1870 with his father, newspaperman and White Mountains historian Frank H. Burt recalled, "We stayed over a week end, having ample time for distinct impressions to sink into my mind of the Old Man, the Cannon, the Flume, the Basin and the Pool."[3] A century on, the Flume was still creating memories. Following a stop at the Old Man of the Mountain, "you and your folks could all go to drink local birch beer and hike in the Flume" recalled one letter-writer to the *New York Times* in 2003, decades after the event.[4] It was an early visit to the Flume that awakened this own writer's interest in the White Mountains and their history.

Nothing can replace a visit to the Flume and the pleasure of experiencing it firsthand. It is therefore hoped that this volume that explores the Flume's recreational heritage will not only fulfill the desire of former Flume director C.T. Bodwell for "a small attractive booklet—one that fully describes the past, present, and also the plans for the future," but will also encourage those who have not visited the Flume to do so and will reawaken fond memories for those who have.[5]

CHAPTER 1

"THERE I WAS IN A REGULAR FLUME"

THE FORMATION AND DISCOVERY OF FLUME GORGE

GEOLOGY

The Flume is located in Lincoln, New Hampshire, at the southern end of Franconia Notch, a pass or gap in the White Mountains between Mount Lafayette on the east and the nearly sheer exfoliating cliffs of Cannon Mountain on the west.[6] Noted for its numerous natural wonders—including the Flume, the Pool, the Basin and, until 2003, the rock profile known as the Old Man of the Mountain—Franconia Notch was described in 1859 by Boston Unitarian clergyman and travel writer Thomas Starr King as "a huge museum of curiosities."[7] Since European Americans first became aware of these "curiosities" two hundred years ago, they have become New Hampshire's leading tourist attractions.

Among the most noteworthy of these is the Flume, where nearly parallel walls of Conway granite extend in length from west to east some eight hundred feet along Flume Brook. Rising to heights of between seventy and ninety feet, these walls range from twelve to twenty feet apart. (In 1850, the narrowness of the Flume was described for cosmopolitan readers as "wide enough apart for, perhaps, two New-York omnibuses, provided New-York drivers managed them.").[8] The bed of the gorge is filled with debris washed down over the centuries while the cliff tops are heavily wooded, providing shade for the rich growth of mosses proliferating on the damp rock walls.

Wesley Carr. *Franconia Notch*, showing the southern end of Franconia Notch in a view looking west from the Franconia Ridge, photograph from Flickr, August 9, 2014. The Flume is located in the foothills at the center of the view.

The Flume's formation began nearly 200 million years ago with the cooling of the subterranean granite that today forms its nearly perpendicular planar walls (or "mural precipices," as state geologist Charles T. Jackson referred to them).[9] Magma forced up through the earth filled the chasm, along with vertical fissures in the surrounding granite, forming a basalt trap dike (a layer of crystallized volcanic rock sandwiched between two layers of older granite) when it cooled. Over millennia, the granite was exposed while the more frangible dike gradually eroded and disintegrated. Continual frost action as water in the fissures behind the face of the walls froze and expanded pried loose fragments of the granite wall, shedding them into the chasm below. Glaciation did relatively little to alter the appearance of the Flume beyond depositing glacial debris in the chasm.[10]

Explorers and visitors, unversed in geology, believed the Flume to have been created through a tremendous earthquake, and this view occasionally resurfaced even after being discredited. Politician and poet Harry Hibbard (1839), Starr King (1859) and Whitefield minister and pamphleteer Guy Roberts (1924) all repeated it.[11] Others claimed that the Flume was the result of erosion. Jackson, who visited as part of the state geological survey in 1843, was unequivocal, however, writing that simple erosion was not the culprit. The Flume, Jackson wrote, "resulted, not from the abrasion of the rocks, caused by the action of running water, but to have been produced

White Mountains Studio. *The Flume, Franconia Notch, White Mts., N.H.*, real photo postcard, circa 1930. *Author's collection.*

Littleton View Company. *Howland's Flume, Mt. Kinsman, N.H.*, albumen silver print stereograph, circa 1870. *Courtesy of the Miriam and Ira D. Wallach Division of Art, Print and Photographs: Photography Collection, New York Public Library.*

originally by a fracture of the uplifted rocks. The walls of the chasm on either hand exhibit proof in favor of this opinion; for they are not water-worn, but present surfaces of fracture."[12]

Jackson was aware of reports of a trap dike at the upper end of the Flume, but his assistants in 1841 were unable to ascertain its location due to the amount of water running in the brook.[13] It was subsequently located and reported by Professor Oliver P. Hubbard in the late 1840s.[14]

Though certainly the most marvelous, the Franconia Notch flume is not the only geological feature of its kind. Several lesser-known flumes exist in the White Mountains, a number of which were discovered during the nineteenth century. The *Nashua Daily Telegraph* in August 1869 reported the find of a flume three times as high but much shorter than the Franconia Notch Flume on Flume Brook near Mad River, as well as two others on the upper part of Mount Willard in Crawford Notch by Professor C.H. Hitchcock in 1875. Howland's Flume on a spur of Mount Kinsman in Easton was opened informally in August 1879 and drew the curious, who disappointingly found it shorter and shallower than its Franconia Notch counterpart. Six years earlier, the *Nashua Daily Telegraph* had similarly characterized the Dixville or "Baby" Flume at Dixville Notch as unremarkable.[15]

DISCOVERY

Regarding the discovery by European Americans of Franconia Notch's Flume, little is actually known. The find is typically attributed to ninety-three-year-old "Aunt" Jess Guernsey, who reputedly stumbled upon the chasm while in search of a better fishing hole in June 1808. It has been stated that due to her disoriented mind, few believed her tale until she brought a local farm boy with her to verify the claim. By the 1930s, the tale had accrued additional layers, including Aunt Jess's marriage to David Guernsey and her Irish origin.

This version of the Flume's discovery has been repeated countless times and has become the accepted orthodox view. Bearing little relation to the facts and challenging the credulity of the listener, the tale continues to appear in works of both a general and a scholarly nature.[16] Though indeed "stranger things have happened," the Guernsey account is more likely folklore embellished over the years rather than historical fact.

The provenance of the tale is murky. The attribution of the find to "Jess Guernsey" seems to have first appeared in Moses Sweetser's 1876 White Mountains guidebook, where the author remarked that "the Flume was discovered by Mrs. Jessie Guernsey, while fishing along the brook."[17] Hamilton Child in his *Gazetteer of Grafton County* (1886) corroborates Sweetser and is more specific, stating that the discoverer was the *wife* of Jesse Guernsey of Sugar Hill (then still part of Lisbon).[18] At the time, it was not unusual for a woman to be referred to by her husband's Christian name, and the children of Mrs. Guernsey's brother-in-law David Guernsey (including Asahel Guernsey, with whom she and Jesse lived for a time) and from whom Sweetser may have heard the tale would have accordingly referred to her as "Aunt Jesse." Notably, neither of these early citations mentions Mrs. Guernsey's age nor the circumstances that brought her into the Flume woods.

Documentary evidence points to Jesse Guernsey's wife, thirty-three-year-old Olive (West) Guernsey, as the discoverer.[19] Jesse had come to New Hampshire from Rehoboth in southeastern Massachusetts, where land shortages and a growing population encouraged the younger generation to migrate to lands in northern New England. First settling at Richmond and later Winchester, New Hampshire, Jesse and his brother David Guernsey settled in the Franconia region by 1800.

The continual repetition of the Guernsey folktale distracts from the more genuine history of the family's continuing relationship with the Flume following 1808 and their participation in the early tourist trade at

Kilburn Brothers. *Flume below the Boulder*, albumen silver print stereograph, circa 1875. The scene here differed little from that of 1808. *Courtesy of the Boston Public Library.*

Franconia Notch. Like the Crawford family at Crawford Notch and other White Mountains families of the era, the Guernseys embraced the new economic opportunity tourism offered at a time when such opportunity in the region was limited.

Guernsey family members continued to reside at the notch, providing accommodation for early Flume visitors and acting as guides. Jesse (1766–1855) and his son John (1795–1868) were licensed in 1837 to conduct a tavern at their home near present-day Indian Head, a mile south of the Flume. In 1841, Francis Parkman described this operation, which had a "rather discouraging aspect," as "the sole tavern and the sole house" at Lincoln.[20] More troubling was that one of the two men—most probably

G.W. Morris. *On the Road to the Flume from No. Woodstock, N.H.*, lithographic postcard, circa 1900. Wayside House gift shop, with postcards and balsam pillows conspicuous among the souvenirs. *Author's collection.*

John, who was termed "innkeeper" in 1837—appears to have been an alcoholic.[21] "We found the host drunk," Parkman recorded in his journal, "and it was with difficulty that we made him comprehend that clean sheets, a couple of chairs, and a table were indispensable requisites." In mid-August 1842, Parkman returned and noted in his journal, "The drunken scoundrel Gurnsey [*sic*] has surrendered his house to one Knight(s), and remains a sort of useless fixture on the premises."[22] Abolitionist Nathaniel Peabody Rogers visited Guernsey's in late August 1841 and encountered the host in the same condition as Parkman had found him. Rogers recorded that "poor Gurnsey [*sic*] was so stupidly besotted when we returned from the Flume" that he was unable to convince Rogers whether the horses he had left there to be refreshed had been watered and fed.[23]

Better regarded by Flume tourists was John's son, farmer Levi E. Guernsey, who continued to reside on the family's notch land and was described as "the best guide in the vicinity" at a rate of three dollars per day.[24] It is probably Levi's wife, Aurilla, who is the Mrs. Guernsey who operated a souvenir stand between the Flume and the Profile House until 1897, when it was relocated a half mile south of the Flume House on the road to North Woodstock. Here she made and sold souvenirs as well as alpenstocks and "maple sugar cakes with walnuts in them."[25]

ANOTHER CLAIMANT

Despite the ubiquity of Olive Guernsey's story, there is another claimant as the discoverer of the Flume. In 1924, the *Nashua Telegraph* attributed the discovery to Allen Thompson (1814–1909), a well-respected nineteenth-century trapper, hunter, guide and later proprietor of the Sportsman's Home in Bethlehem.[26] Setting out one warm December day from North Woodstock to cross Mount Lafayette, Thompson discovered the tracks of a large bear as the weather turned and it began to snow. Following the tracks down the mountain and into a gorge along a stream, Thompson was forced to take shelter in an eighteen-by-twelve-foot cave as dusk settled and the storm worsened. Thompson later recalled:

> *The morning after the storm I stepped out to see the most beautiful sight. There I was in a regular flume, walls straight on either side, and just above, a picturesque water-fall rushing over a precipice in a perfect sheet and splashing on the rocks below. The sun shining on the spray, the drifts*

Profile Wonder Shops, Profile and Flume Hotels Co. *The Bear Cave at Top of the Flume, Franconia Notch, N.H.*, lithographic postcard, circa 1920. It was in this cave that Allen Thompson allegedly sheltered before his "discovery" of the Flume. *Author's collection.*

> *of snow and the swiftness of the stream were great. I glanced at it for a while, then went down, dreaming how I would build a road up to it some day and make a fortune.*[27]

Though Thompson's recollections do not specifically state that it was the Franconia Notch Flume in which he sheltered, the *Telegraph* explicitly makes that connection. Thompson, however, was not present in the White Mountains until about the mid-1830s, by which time the Flume had apparently already reached public notice. Regardless of which pioneer truly discovered the Flume, news traveled slowly, and it is more than possible that the Flume was "discovered" on multiple occasions by area residents who were unaware of its presence and had failed to hear earlier news of its finding.

CHAPTER 2

"AS WILD A PIECE OF SCENERY AS I EVER CHANCED TO SEE"

THE SUBLIME FLUME, 1826–1850

EARLIEST TOURISTS

The Flume was slower to develop than attractions near the White Mountain (Crawford) Notch, in part due to its inaccessibility. Efforts to construct a roadway from the south through Franconia Notch to improve communication with the New Hampshire Iron Factory Company at Franconia were undertaken after that company's incorporation in 1805, but the roadway remained rudimentary for years. Following a New Hampshire legislative appropriation in 1826, the road was improved and was subsequently described as tolerable.[28] Two years later, artist Thomas Cole termed it "good."[29] Though improvement of the roadway permitted regular mail stage service between Plymouth and Franconia, Franconia Notch itself remained practically deserted.

Adventurous tourists, however, were undeterred by the region's isolation, and Franconia Notch began to draw a trickle of visitors from New England's educated and cultured elite who read about the notch beginning with an account in the September 9 and 16, 1826 editions of the *New Hampshire Statesman and Concord Register*. According to White Mountains historian Frederick W. Kilbourne, author Nathaniel Hawthorne "doubtless" visited Franconia Notch (but probably not the Flume) in 1832, though an unidentified Dartmouth College senior *did* visit both the Flume and the nearby Pool in 1837 and found them largely unchanged when he revisited forty-one years

Kilburn Brothers. *Flume below the Boulder*, albumen silver print stereograph, circa 1867. *Author's collection.*

later in August 1878.[30] Another Dartmouth graduate, politician and poet Harry Hibbard, also likely visited the gorge prior to the publication of his poem "Franconia Mountain Notch" in the *Democratic Review* in April 1839.[31]

Ralph Waldo Emerson visited in the summer of 1839 and wrote to Margaret Fuller of his impressions of the Flume:

> *I went to see what is called "The Flume" as wild a piece of scenery as I ever chanced to see though the describable facts are nothing but a small stream pouring through a granite ravine over which at one point a natural bridge is made by a big stone which has fallen in to the top of the chasm. But we*

> *lowlanders so rarely see the aboriginal forest that here where it is in wildest wonder & strength it enobles the strange spectacle & really healed me who set out from Littleton that morning a sick man & doubtful whether I could crawl after my party, for we walked a mile in to the woods at this point.*[32]

Just weeks later, Henry David Thoreau and his brother John visited the Flume and the Pool, with Thoreau noting tersely in his journal on September 7, 1839, "In Lincoln visited Stone Flume."[33] Though Thoreau failed to record his impressions of the Flume, they were indelible; thirteen years later when he was shown botanical specimens gathered there by Concord neighbor Elizabeth Hoar, memories flooded back. "The [lily of the valley berries], red-ripe, hanging from the axils of the leaves, affected me, reminding me of the progress of autumn in the north; and the other two were a very fit importation, still dripping with the moisture, the water, of the Flume. It carries you, indeed, into the primitive wood. To think how, in those wild woods, now hang these wild berries, in grim solitude as of yore."[34]

Francis Parkman visited Franconia Notch in the company of his family in 1838 and again with his Harvard classmate Daniel Denison Slade in 1841, when they specifically sought out the Flume. "The Flume had acquired some notoriety, having been seen and described by a comparatively large number of visitors," and the pair were anxious to see it.[35] On July 29, the pair bushwhacked through the forest and along the Pemigewasset River. Parkman refused the guide, and as a consequence, the pair could not locate the chasm. "Hang your dirty Flume! I move we go back to the house and get the old man to show us the way as he said he would," Slade complained. "I wish we had never come."[36] The following day, this time accompanied by a guide, the pair successfully located the object of their search. Parkman later recorded in his journal that visitors seldom attempted to locate the Flume unaided, and "when they did they usually returned discouraged and frightened, or else became lost and had to be searched for with shoutings and firings of guns."[37] The pair also visited the nearby Pool, which would long be associated with the Flume, and which Slade noted "was then almost inaccessible, and had been seen by few, if any, travellers before ourselves;

Francis Parkman, photographic print from original daguerreotype, circa 1843. *Author's collection.*

J. Whitney. *Flume, Franconia*, in C.T. Jackson, *Final Report on the Geology and Mineralogy of the State of New Hampshire*, 1844. *Author's collection.*

its existence even was scarcely known to the most hardy woodsman."[38] A month following Parkman and Slade, abolitionist Nathaniel Peabody Rogers visited in late August 1841 but sensibly used the footpath through the dense woods.

By the end of the 1840s, public awareness of the Flume had become widespread. The *Salem* (Massachusetts) *Register* considered it "one of the greatest natural curiosities of our country," a characterization reprinted in papers across the nation.[39] Numerous travelers' accounts of the Flume appeared in nationally circulated newspapers and journals, including the widely read *Harper's* in 1852. By the late 1850s, these accounts had become so commonplace as to elicit the remark from the *Congregationalist* that "we have seen [in the White Mountains] only what it falls to the lot of many to see, and what has been described so often as to make a repetition of the tale weary to those familiar with it."[40] Descriptions also became less necessary following 1844, when the Flume was first depicted pictorially, an image appearing in Jackson's *Final Report on the Geology and Mineralogy of the State of New Hampshire.*

ROMANTIC AND INTELLECTUAL VIEWS OF THE FLUME

Visits by eminent thinkers who subsequently discussed and shared their experiences helped romanticize and intellectualize the Flume during the antebellum period. A coterie of New England intellectuals, many Harvard- and Dartmouth-educated, viewed the Flume through the lens of their own philosophical, theological, artistic and literary beliefs and in the process helped create a cultural vision of Franconia Notch that would subsequently influence the twentieth-century conservation movement in New Hampshire.

For this educated elite, the Flume was considered an example of the sublime, an aesthetic and later literary concept originating with Edmund Burke in the previous century that defined the sublime as that which evoked feelings of awe, pain, danger and terror. In contrast to the rational, the sublime was a purely emotional response and could be found in the wildness and grandeur of untamed nature. In the midst of this wilderness, man could understand himself within the context of God's universe, an experience that could prove overpowering and terrifying, yet thrilling.[41]

Early nineteenth-century Romantics became fascinated with the sublime and sought to discover it in nature and depict it in poetry, art and literature. Sublime nature was something to be admired and studied, a view that encouraged visitors to seek out—and ultimately exalt—the Flume.

The earliest visitors invoked the language of the sublime and termed the chasm awe-inspiring (or "awful" in the language of the period).[42] Words including "wild" were perpetually and unrestrainedly used to describe the Flume and its surrounding scenery. An unidentified Yale undergraduate, fully versed in the vocabulary of the sublime, visited in 1843 and was enraptured. "The Flume is very wildness!" he exclaimed. "The channel is perfectly awful! It varies from four to ten feet in width, with perpendicular sides of ragged granite from ten to fifty feet in length. This surpasses all the mountain scenery in awful wildness!"[43] Another visitor was equally taken, remarking that "the beholder is struck with amazement, wonder, and awe; and involuntarily exclaims, 'How wondrous are thy works, O God!' and sinks into insignificance before the sublimity of nature."[44] Author, artist and explorer Charles Lanman was "astonished" when in 1844 he first viewed the Flume, "the centre of as perfect and holy a wilderness of scenery as could be imagined," while a correspondent in 1865 similarly was struck by the chasm's "wild grandeur and sublimity."[45]

Mythological and religious overtones also colored early descriptions of the Flume. One chronicler recalled the Flume as "overshadowed by sombre foliage, the whole scene wild, dark, and dank, with a stream of almost Styx-like blackness pouring into the black abyss below,—the very spot where the ancients would inevitably have sought an opening to the infernal regions."[46] Other visitors described the Flume in more orthodoxly religious, almost reverential tones. "Scripturally inclined tourists have likened the Flume to the valley of the shadow of death," noted one commentator in 1879, while another in 1853 compared a visit to worship in a temple.[47] As late as 1935, it was written of the Flume that "there is something ecclesiastical about this forest crypt—a sublimity and an awfulness."[48]

Others were unable to find adequate words to describe the Flume. The editor of the *National Era* simply stated that it was "perhaps the most wonderful thing in the mountain. We shall attempt no description; all we have to say is, go and see."[49] The Reverend F.D. Chandler agreed, noting that "language fails to convey to the reader any correct idea of the sublime beauty of the scenery" of the Flume.[50] The consensus was that the Flume needed to be visited to be truly experienced. "With a vivid imagination [the Flume] can be *seen* by the 'view,' but this work of nature must be *felt* to

William James Hubbard. *The Angler* (Portrait of Charles Lanman), oil on canvas, 1846. *Courtesy of High Museum of Art.*

be well seen. Proud and pygmy man needs to measure himself in such a presence as the Flume."[51]

Over time, regard for the Flume as a sublime scene would fade, overwhelmed by the sheer number of visitors coming for an experience that was less thoughtful and more social. Intellectuals became dismayed when newer visitors whom they perceived as less cultivated began to regard the Flume

The Flume, real photo postcard, circa 1915. *Author's collection.*

principally for its social opportunities rather than its spiritual or intellectual associations. So palpable was this shift that newspaper correspondents were able to document it as it was happening. One southern correspondent in 1852 employing the classic language of the sublime characterized the Flume as a scene "of terrific grandeur [which] produces a feeling of desolation, as if entering the damp and gloomy cavern of despair." He quickly noted, however, that this bleakness was soon dispelled by a group of young married Connecticut women who "clambered merrily over the rough and steep rocks," apparently oblivious to the "awfulness" surrounding them.[52] Another writer for the *Brooklyn Eagle* would have a similar experience in 1879. Writing of the Flume in almost spiritual terms, he revealed his contempt for one visitor he apparently felt did not have the intellect to appreciate it:

> *To stand on the narrow plank that separates you from the mountain stream which rushes over the rocky bed at the bottom, pressed against the dark, damp wall, and look up with awe struck eyes to the mighty pendant pass which threatens momentarily to fall on the defenseless head, is an experience hardly adapted to the festal mood of a pleasure party. One pretty creature, who flitted through the sombre place like a strayed butterfly, spoke more truly than her little soul could comprehend when she pronounced it "Just too awfully lovely!"*[53]

GETTING TO THE FLUME

Regardless of the reasons that drew people to it, the Flume was made more readily accessible to visitors following the arrival in 1850 of the Boston, Concord & Montreal Railroad (BC&M) at Plymouth, twenty-five miles to the south. Railroads like the BC&M democratized travel and in so doing laid the foundation for the development of the tourist industry not only in Franconia Notch but in the White Mountains as a whole. This change occurred virtually overnight, as indicated by a report dating from 1851:

> *Time was when Northern New Hampshire and Vermont were considered out of the country. The principal, and in fact the only point of attraction for summer tourists, were the White Mountains, and those were reached only by days of travel in lumbering stage coaches or private carriages. And it was only the more wealthy men that could afford to make the journey, and the*

> *more hardy and resolute that dared the undertaking....But Time changes all things. The iron horse is daily heard snorting through the deep ravines of the Switzerland of America, in summer dragging car after car load of pleasure and health seeking travellers, who are bent on breathing the pure air of the mountains rather than the nauseous vapors of low lands.*[54]

The BC&M nearly immediately began advertising its connections to the White Mountains, and by 1859, possible routes to the tourist regions from New York were so numerous as to prompt the characterization by the *New York Herald* that they were as "thick as the raspberries between this [city] and the Flume."[55] Lillian Foster, writing in August 1858, agreed regarding the ease of travel from New York and was surprised that more people did not visit the region, though she acknowledged that their hesitancy stemmed largely from a lingering perception of the White Mountains as being difficult to reach.[56]

With the opening of the BC&M, the journey from Boston to Plymouth was reduced to five and a half hours, making the Flume easily reachable in a day. No longer was "the undertaking...mighty, owing to its distance, nor fearful on account of the fatigue of travel."[57]

From Plymouth, visitors in 1850 were conveyed in a four-horse stage that left daily at two o'clock in the afternoon and arrived at the Flume twenty-four miles away at six o'clock in the evening.[58] A traveler on one of these in July 1850 reported, "The day of our journey was very hot, but the horses were driven through at a killing pace, nevertheless. Of either horses or coaches on this route, there can be no complaint. They are of the best class."[59] Lillian Foster in 1858 found the stage ride to the Flume from Plymouth the most pleasant part of her journey, noting the gradually enclosing mountain walls, the variegated scenery and the presence of the nearby Pemigewasset.[60] In 1857, six-horse stages ran between Plymouth and Littleton north of Franconia Notch three times weekly, with three additional trips each week during the peak season of July, August and September, with stops for the Flume. One savvy traveler advised riding on the outside seats of these stages or in open wagons in order to better admire the view.[61]

While the railroad facilitated travel to New Hampshire, some still found the journey so trying that they resolved to vacation elsewhere. "By the time the tourist reaches the Franconia Notch he feels that for him the pleasures of this Switzerland of America are ended—that his warfare with packhorses and guides is accomplished—that it becomes his duty to inquire his way to Saratoga and turn his face thitherward."[62] Nonetheless, many did endure the

Enoch Wood Perry. *The Pemigewasset Coach*, oil on canvas, circa 1899. *The Shelburne Museum, Vermont.*

often tiring journey, equipped with much baggage. Packed within trunks and valises was the suggested outfit for the 1850s-era tourist, including "a good stock of linen, warm under clothes, over coats, shawls, stout shoes or rubbers, a straw hat and cap, leaving the awkward dress hat at home, and as much superfluous dress clothing as possible. Umbrellas and stout walking canes are useful, and should not be forgotten."[63] The warm clothing protected against unexpected morning showers and the chill of evening. Visitors to the Flume were also cautioned to bring along their "waterproof" (raincoat) in order to protect against dampness while climbing through the gorge.[64]

THE FLUME HOUSE

As with other scenic attractions in the White Mountains, a hotel was established near the Flume in the second quarter of the nineteenth century to provide accommodations for those wishing to visit. The Flume House would ultimately be owned in common with the gorge and would become closely associated with the Flume. In attempting to fill its rooms, the Flume House's owners would foster the Flume's development as a tourist attraction and inaugurate commercialized recreation in Franconia Notch.

New Hampshire resort hotels like the Flume House were among the earliest in the nation established to take advantage solely of the landscape, and they would revolutionize the nature-seeking experience. Strategically situated, not only did they help popularize and develop nearby natural attractions, but they also allowed guests to explore nature without the difficulty, danger and lack of comforts experienced by the earliest tourists. As a result, attractions like the Flume with its carriage road and boardwalk abetted carefully arranged forays into nature, which was made more accessible to the general public (and consequently less sublime). No longer would a visit to the Flume be either daunting or dangerous. The Flume House, like other mid-nineteenth-century examples of this phenomenon in the White Mountains, including the Glen House, Crawford House, Fabyan House and Profile House, became well known and patronized as the number of visitors drawn to view the scenery skyrocketed.[65]

At the time, Crawford Notch with its accessibility to Mount Washington was the locus of tourism in the White Mountains region. Starr King, however, argued the favorability of Franconia over Crawford Notch. While conceding in 1859 that the latter perhaps had the more dramatic scenery, he found it oppressive. He maintained that Crawford was scarred by landslides, the mountains little forested and the site overpowering and in the end unwelcoming for a long stay.[66] Mrs. M.E. Blake also indicated her preference for Franconia Notch when she remarked, "What was but suggestion at Crawford's is reality here."[67] English sociologist and writer Harriet Martineau described Franconia Notch simply as "the noblest mountain pass I saw in the United States."[68]

Sojourners like Starr King who favored Franconia Notch lacked unanimity on which end was most scenic, though many preferred the southern end in the vicinity of the Flume where views were more expansive.[69] The need for an inn at this location consequently was advocated, the absence of any suitable habitation as late as 1846 being remarked upon.

The early history of the hostelries in Franconia Notch, including the Flume House, is not well documented. As noted earlier, the Guernsey family conducted a tavern about a mile south of the Flume in the 1830s and early 1840s. In February 1841, Jesse and John Guernsey, likely overwhelmed by debt, sold their tavern and one-hundred-acre farm, which the following year passed into the hands of Benjamin Knight (1796–1858) of Bath, New Hampshire. Parkman in mid-August 1842 notes Knight as the owner but indicates that the Guernseys remained on as employees.[70]

To Knight must be attributed the Flume's earliest development as a tourist attraction. Desiring to attract travelers to the region and recognizing the opportunity that a location closer to the Flume would afford, Knight constructed a new inn he named the Flume House near the present-day Liberty Springs trailhead parking area. Opened on July 4, 1846, the inn advertised the scenic sites in the vicinity and, in taking the name of the Flume, wedded itself to the chasm as an attraction of note. This connection was intended to promote the business of the hotel, and for decades the Flume would be used as the draw that would help fill the Flume House's rooms. In all, Knight is said to have been an innkeeper successfully for about five years until the Flume House was destroyed by fire.[71] Knight sold the property in two successive deeds in 1847 and 1848 to Ira Coffin of New Hampton, who ultimately entered into partnership with Benjamin Kenney of Bethlehem after acquiring the property in its entirety.[72]

FLUME HOUSE.

BENJAMIN KNIGHT

FLUME.

CASCADE.

POOL.

BASIN.

"THE OLD MAN OF THE MOUNTAIN,"

Flume House, broadside, 1846. *Author's collection.*

To manage a rebuilt hotel that opened the last day of June 1849, Coffin and Kenney engaged Richard A. Taft (1812–1881), proprietor of the Washington House hotel at Lowell. Taft, who, like Knight, perceived the tourist potential of Franconia Notch, was ultimately responsible for its success as a tourist destination, and "to him more than to any other man is due the development of the conveniences and comforts which attend[ed] a summer journey to the mountains of New Hampshire" in the mid-1800s.[73]

In 1849, Taft advertised this "new and commodious House, situated at the Flume and Pool," which had the advantage of being reachable from Boston by tea time the same day.[74] Though one commentator described the hotel in July 1850 as a "hastily-built caravansers" (caravansary), implying that it had improved little upon earlier accommodations and drew a lower-class crowd, the *Boston Daily Atlas* maintained that "those who know, say that a better place cannot be found to obtain comfort and enjoyment during a visit" to the White Mountains.[75] This reputation was attributable to changes inaugurated by Taft (who was admitted into partnership with Coffin and Kenney in January 1852).[76] Based on his analysis of the earliest Flume House register, researcher John Gath agreed that there was a dramatic shift

John B. Heywood. *Flume House*, albumen silver print stereograph, circa 1860. *Courtesy of the Miriam and Ira D. Wallach Division of Art, Print and Photographs: Photography Collection, New York Public Library.*

to a better class of trade in the early 1850s. "This change is so radical as to suggest the possibility that not only was the character of the patronage different, but that, indeed, the house itself might also have been."[77]

Helping to attract visitors was the Flume House's location proximate to the Flume with admirable views in multiple directions, particularly southward over the Pemigewasset Valley, what Edward Everett Hale termed "the matchless southern prospect from the Flume House."[78] Starr King described the view from the hotel as one of "perpetual refreshment" and wrote in the flowing prose of the era of its beauties. Of particular note were the ever-changing light and shadows of the southern notch, with colors of the forested hills and mountains shifting from green to amethyst to "glorious purple." Starr King argued that in no other location could "the fever...be taken more gently and cunningly out of a worried or burdened brain."[79] By 1852, the Flume House had grown to be a three-story building 262 feet in length with two-story piazzas on the southern and eastern sides. Its one hundred rooms accommodated over four hundred visitors over the course of seventy days in the summer of 1852.[80]

Among White Mountain resorts, the Flume House was considered tasteful and elegant, and many considered it *the* "resort of wealth and fashion, hardly equaled by any other hotel among the mountains."[81] Dr. Gamaliel Bailey Jr., editor of the abolitionist newspaper the *National Era* and a guest of the hotel for several seasons in the 1850s, wrote, "The Flume House is quite a considerable affair, with a fine table, and a parlor as large as a concert-room, which, the evening we were there, was adorned with any number of fashionable people, in full dress, (from Boston we presume,) stuck up all around the walls, like frames in a picture gallery."[82] Another guest from August 1853 described a more homely experience, noting clusters of families and travelers engaged in genial conversation in the hotel parlor, coupled with instrumental music and vocal selections at interludes.[83] One entertainment frequently noted was provided by two hotel employees masquerading as a Burmese elephant. The act "shook the ceiling with laughter that its natural antics produced."[84] As late as 1854, many argued that the Flume House was the most popular of the summer resorts.[85] In addition to Bailey, the hotel's clientele included Starr King (1849), Daniel Webster (1849, 1851), publisher James T. Fields (1851), future president Franklin Pierce (1851) and politician Richard Henry Dana Jr. (1854), better known for his 1840 memoir, *Two Years before the Mast*.[86]

Southworth & Hawes. *Franklin Pierce*, photographic print from original daguerreotype, circa 1852. *Author's collection.*

Yet while originally fashionable, the Flume House was soon eclipsed by the Profile House, which Taft opened at the northern end of the notch in 1853 and which by 1858 was considered the grander of the two. Ads carried as late as 1859 nonetheless still gave top billing to the Flume House.[87]

THE NEW TOURIST

While rising affluence in New England in the mid-nineteenth century promoted steadily increasing visitation to the Flume, establishment of the Flume House helped alter tourist habits, discouraging the sedentariness that had been a hallmark of the Northeast's resorts and welcoming the arrival of a more active visitor. Previously, "all creation went to Saratoga, to exchange their lassitude for a belly-full of Congress water.... Saratoga is visited by invalids, made so by an undue indulgence in the fashionable follies and vices of high life, and they spend their nights in dances and intrigues, their mornings in bed and afternoons in guzzling bilge water. New-Hampshire... [is] the resort of those who scorn this—those who go there love to look on the handiwork of the great Creator, and love to enjoy the air and exercise of the Mountains."[88] While the characterization of the popular New York resort may have been unfair, the concept emerged that a tour of the White Mountains was intended to be vigorous, replete with regular activity and appetite-inducing outdoor exercise.

Another change effected by the Flume House and other large resort hotels of the era was the rise in popularity of week-long or season-long stays. "Things are changing," wrote the *National Era* in 1854. "People are beginning to learn that the longer they linger in the mountains, the more reluctant they grow to quit them."[89] The Flume House tapped into this reluctance by offering a variety of attractions and diversions to maintain the interest of guests.

To encourage extended stays, the Flume House included a reading room, two "very fine" bowling alleys and a livery.[90] Opposite the hotel, "in a place disassociated from scenes of merriment," Taft constructed a fifty-foot-square Gothic-style wooden white-painted chapel for Sunday worship about 1853.[91] Nearby, visits could be had to the Basin (yet another of Franconia Notch's several natural attractions), ascents could be made up Mount Lafayette on horseback or on foot up Mount Pemigewasset and drives could be taken through the notch to the Profile House over "an undulating but good road."[92] In 1854, a writer for the *Boston Evening Transcript* reflected this growing desire for newer attractions and, though satisfied with revisiting the Flume, Pool, Basin and Old Man, was pleased with the opening of a new attraction, the Mount Lafayette bridle trail.[93]

This need to provide a large variety of diversions also encouraged the search for new attractions, which was occasionally rewarded. On August 20, 1855, the editor of the *New Hampshire Democrat*, writing from the Flume

John B. Heywood. *View from Flume House*, albumen silver print stereograph, circa 1860. *The Miriam and Ira D. Wallach Division of Art, Print and Photographs: Photography Collection, New York Public Library.*

House, announced the discovery of a new scenic delight nearby, the Basin Cascades. "Since our former visit here a new attraction has been added to this part of the mountains. Some forty yards west from the famous Basin has been discovered a magnificent combination of cascade, waterfall, flume, and cataract, extending a full mile, and presenting a succession of panoramas beyond the effort of pen or pencil."[94] Georgianna (Harvard) Falls was added to the list of discoveries in 1858, as were Lonesome Lake (1871) and Bridal Veil Falls on Coppermine Brook (1886).[95]

The Flume House also emphasized the social aspect of travel, previously a solitary activity engaged in by individuals or very small groups. English writer and botanist Lady Amelia Murray, who spent nearly a week at the Flume House and twice visited the Flume in August 1856, noted the "large and heterogeneous…society accidentally gathered together" in the hotel parlors. She remarked upon the guests' "good humour and propriety.…All converse without introduction, yet I have seen nothing like forwardness or vulgarity of manner: though there is a *degree* of restraint and stiffness, I find myself much more at home than I should be in any hotel, either on the Continent of Europe or in the British Isles—it is more like the freedom of a very large country-house in England. This peculiarity of American manners I have never heard mentioned—and it is certainly a striking one."[96]

While much has been written about the impact of the White Mountains' grand hotels on upper-class vacation habits and their encouragement of a new type of vacationer who remained for an entire season, the concurrently increasing numbers of more transient tourists, largely from the middle class, who were also making their way to the mountains should not be overlooked. Many of these visitors reflected the tendencies of hurried tourists of the present day, briefly visiting the most attractions in as short a time as possible. "Few thought of lingering among them," noted an 1854 correspondent. "The object was to pass over the beaten track, from one prominent point to another, staying just long enough to catch a glimpse at each."[97] Richard Henry Dana Jr. was one such tourist, visiting the Profile, the Basin and the Flume in quick succession on July 13, 1854. Dana and his party walked to the very top of the Flume and, like many before and since, had the misfortune of getting caught in a summer rainstorm. "Just as we were at the top of the Flume, as far as we [could] be [from] our carriage, a heavy thunder shower came up. We were obliged to walk back, [about] ½ mile to our carriage & ride another ½ mile, in a soaking rain to the Flume House, where we took rooms & got properly dried & refitted."[98]

The presence of these passing tourists encouraged hoteliers to take the most advantage of their brief stay, or so believed one tourist who complained of the expense of coach rides to the Flume from the Profile House. "Of course bills are high and necessarily so as the season is compressed into two months [but]...it is not at the high bills we complain...[but of the] unconscionable charge for a seat to the 'Flume' [which] is not only two prices for a six miles ride—at which we would not cavil—but it is beyond all bounds of fair, honest, dealing."[99]

The Flume House successfully exploited its location in the midst of such attractions. One guest, writing in the *New York Evening Post* in 1854, remarked, "I know of no hotel more fitted for a protracted resort during the heat of the summer than the Flume House, not only from its vicinity to various interesting localities and its numerous paths for riding and walking among some of the most attractive scenery at the White Hills, but from the excellence of its household arrangements."[100]

Despite these attractions and the new amenities the Flume House offered, the Flume remained the principal draw for tourists, and a visit, according to the *Chicago Tribune*, was considered a must "by all tourists who desire to be considered thorough 'doers' of places of note."[101] No visit to the White Mountains was considered complete without touring the Flume.

CHAPTER 3

"IT NEEDS A VERY SURE FOOT AND STEADY HEAD"

A VISIT TO THE FLUME AND POOL, 1850s

THE APPROACH

For those who visited the Flume during the mid-nineteenth century, the gorge was accessed by means of a narrow footpath branching from the notch road opposite the site of the Flume House. Abolitionist writer and editor Nathaniel Peabody Rogers described this approach as he found it in 1841:

> *The way was exceedingly romantic. It was a footpath through the very deepest and heaviest growth of New Hampshire woods. We passed birches as big as most pines. About a quarter of a mile from the high road, the path pitched down two or three hundred feet very precipitously. At the bottom roared a mountain stream among the rocks* [the Pemigewasset River], *as clear as crystal and as cold as a well. Our way lay across it, on the trunk of a fallen spruce that required some steadiness to pass. We crossed this stream three or four times more and came to the cascade* [Table Rock].[102]

Geologist Charles T. Jackson advised travelers to proceed on foot given the number of small streams that needed to be crossed by means of fallen trees.[103] New Hampshireman Benjamin Brown French, clerk of the United States House of Representatives, followed a path from Knight's tavern on July 1, 1845, which ran "over hills & through valleys, & is rough enough."

The Flume, silver print photograph, circa 1895. *Courtesy of the Upper Pemigewasset Historical Society.*

Hemmed in by underbrush, the path required an eight-year-old boy to guide the party, and the excursion resulted in torn dresses and scratched hands.[104] The boy was likely Benjamin Knight's son, Andrew Jackson Knight, who would "stand on his head at the top beside the Flume Gorge to make the tourists stare."[105]

By 1850, Rogers's winding footpath had been improved into a wagon road suitable for carryalls that conveyed tourists a considerable distance into the woods before having to be abandoned and the occupants' journey resumed on foot.[106] It is possible that further road improvement was undertaken by Taft for the 1853 season when it was reported that he was operating an "elegant new open carriage" with a capacity of twenty drawn by six cream-colored horses to convey passengers to the Flume.[107]

While the Flume represented the principal attraction and most visitors hurried on in anticipation of viewing it, some appreciated the Pemigewasset at the foot of the Flume road for its pleasant scenery, rushing water and more. Nathaniel L. Bowditch of Boston, an enthusiast of swimming in New Hampshire's invigorating waters, in August 1856 climbed among the river's boulders before finding an isolated pool some five feet deep. "I never plunged into water of more icy coldness," Bowditch later remarked.[108] Few others found such a chilling bath pleasurable.

TABLE ROCK

After crossing the river and hiking a short distance, visitors encountered the large, smooth, gently inclined ledge known today as Table Rock. Here an exposed portion of Conway granite of some 37,500 square feet forms the granite floor of Flume Brook, its undulating wave-like surface worn smooth over centuries. Over Table Rock, the pitch of which was likened by some mid-nineteenth-century visitors to that of a house roof, the waters of Flume Brook, during periods of high streamflow, widen and pour in a broad, shallow, sparkling sheet once known as the Cascade.[109] Some observers at the time disputed this name for the fall. "This does not seem to deserve this name [of Cascade]. But when a freshet occurs we conceive that the rush of a heavy volume of water down the long slope of granite, washed smooth for two hundred feet in length and forty feet in width, would be fearfully sublime, but rather more of a cataract than a cascade. As we found it, and as it is in ordinary times, there was a smooth, thin, clear rivulet, gliding noiselessly down the declivity, leaving here and there little basins scooped out of the rock."[110]

Nineteenth-century visitors described the waters descending over Table Rock as transparent, thin and gelatin-like. Starr King described them as "thin, wide, even sheets of crystal colorlessness."[111] One 1859 visitor, enchanted with the scene, remarked that "this water-fall—rather, water-slide—is one of the most fascinating features of these mountain attractions. The water laughs as it courses down the polished plane, it prattles rapidly along the shelving rocks, and it leaps merrily over stone or stick that has fallen on its bed. It is a witching water fall, and tempts the visitor to paddle in its delicious coolness, even to the risk of a horizontal bath in its fairy flood."[112]

Originally there was no path here, and visitors walked directly up the rock's surface. "We walked up, dry shod, the whole length of the cascade," recalled Nathaniel Peabody Rogers in 1841, "to where the rocks begin to wall up on each side, and form the entrance way to the flume."[113] Walking directly on Table Rock permitted visitors another pleasure, that of sampling Flume Brook's waters. Henrietta Payne-Westbrook and her companions took the opportunity on a visit in the late 1880s to dip "ungloved hands in the little hollows where the water gathered deepest, and [drink] a fluid clear and of undoubted purity."[114]

C.T. Bodwell. *Table Rock, Flume, White Mts., N.H.*, real photo postcard, 1933. *Author's collection.*

Entrance to the Flume [Table Rock], albumen silver print stereograph, circa 1860. *Courtesy of the Miriam and Ira D. Wallach Division of Art, Print and Photographs: Photography Collection, New York Public Library.*

Though Table Rock was frequently compared to a slide, those who put it to that use received a jarring ride. One who did (unintentionally) was a Mr. Bartlett, a member of Benjamin Brown French's party who in July 1845 tossed a large rock into the Cascade in order to observe its progress over the ledge. "The effort caused his feet to slide & away he went, following the stone on its downward course; for a short distance he slid, then he commenced running, then down he came, & away into the pool below. We all stood in silence till he got out on the opposite side, drenched from head to foot, then we gave a shout that made the old forest ring again. Miss Bartlett was very much frightened, & when I discovered it I felt really sorry I had indulged in such a laugh, but it was a scene too rich to pass *seriously* over, & Bartlett, with a few scratches on his hands, & some very serious rents in his clothes, joined as heartily & merrily in the laugh as any of us."[115] A Mr. G.K. Goodwin similarly lost his footing in August 1856 and slipped ninety feet down the rock, surfacing in the small pool below. It was recorded that his watch, lost in the accident, was recovered.[116]

THE FLUME

Mid-nineteenth-century descriptions of the Flume proper are innumerable. One writer for the *Boston Evening Transcript*, aware of their number, simply noted, "I am not going to say anything about the scenery around the mountains; no intelligent person can approach the White Mountains without being impressed by the grandeur and beauty of the scenery, but it has been thoroughly described, and I can add nothing that would be new."[117]

Referred to as a "chasm," a "gorge," a "cleft" and a "room" in the rock, the Flume struck immediate awe in visitors upon seeing it. Although the Flume could be walked dry during periods of low water, to accommodate visitors, crude plank walkways (some later fitted with horizontal cleats to provide better footing) along with bridges and steps were installed along the course of Flume Brook, which as late as 1865 remained unnamed.[118] One of the earliest descriptions of these "boardwalks" was left by Swedish author Frederika Bremer, who visited during August 1850: "Along the front of one of the walls our host, in true Yankee fashion, had carried a pathway formed of pieces of timber, stones, branches which did not resemble anything, but along which people, to their astonishment, could walk quite safely, and without the least difficulty, if they steadied themselves with one hand against the rock wall."[119] Just a few days prior to Bremer's visit, the walkway had been extended an additional fifty feet nearer the suspended boulder.

Later in the decade, by the time Starr King visited, the Flume's walkways had been improved, including the addition of primitive railings.

> *We go up, stepping from rock to rock, now walking along a little plank pathway, now mounting by some rude steps, here and there crossing from*

Above: Detroit Publishing Company. *The Flume Looking Up*, glass negative, circa 1900. The boardwalk half a century earlier would have been more rudimentary. *Courtesy of the Library of Congress.*

Opposite: Fred W. Rand. *The Flume*, silver print photograph, 1907. The "little plank pathway" survived into the twentieth century. *Courtesy of the Upper Pemigewasset Historical Society.*

Keystone View Company. *The Flume after a Rain, White Mountains, New Hampshire, U.S.A.*, showing typical springtime damage to the boardwalk, albumen silver print stereograph, 1905. *Courtesy of the Library of Congress.*

> *side to side of the ravine by primitive little bridges, that bend under the feet and that are railed by birch-poles, and then climbing the rocks again, while the spray break upon us from the dashing and roaring stream, till we arrive at a little bridge which spans the narrowest part of the ravine.*[120]

Sophia Thoreau, the writer's younger sister, described the walkways during her 1870 visit as a "'platform' through the gorge."[121]

Climbing through the Flume, which included steadying oneself on the rock wall or occasionally stepping into Flume Brook, could be both slippery and wet. Percy Curtiss, author of the 1874 children's book *Sloppy Dingle*, emphasized that "it is necessary to wear water-proof cloaks and rubber boots in making this excursion."[122]

While the Flume's walkways eliminated the need to scramble over wet rocks, they were not removed seasonally, as they were later, and they appear not to have been consistently maintained, as repairs were frequent. When walkways needed replacement, trees at the top of the chasm walls were simply cut and rolled into the Flume below, according to William B. Swett, who worked on the 1865 repair crew.[123]

THE SUSPENDED BOULDER

Considered the most remarkable among the features of the Flume was the large egg-shaped boulder that was lodged between the chasm's perpendicular walls some fifteen feet overhead. New Hampshire state geologist C.H. Hitchcock estimated its dimensions as fifteen by twelve by eight feet.[124] Richard Taft's later partner Colonel Charles H. Greenleaf maintained that the boulder had likely come to lodge between the Flume walls by the same force that would remove it in 1883—a spring freshet or flood accompanied by a mountain slide. Hitchcock surmised that it was a glacial erratic of Franconia breccia carried from Eagle Cliff, four miles distant, prior to the creation of the Flume.[125]

Regardless of how the boulder arrived at the Flume and came to be suspended in its peculiar predicament, its presence made nearly all tourists who passed beneath it shudder. Starr King described the boulder even as "unpleasant to look at, if the nerves are irresolute."[126] Photographer F.B. Gage quickened his steps when passing beneath for fear that the boulder would crash and crush him underneath, and others exhibited similar feelings of timidity.[127] "Some will not venture there, arguing that as the rock is sure to fall *some* time, it is just as likely to come down when they are under it as at any other period," rationalized one cautious visitor.[128]

References to the Sword of Damocles, which represented imminent peril, seemed inevitable and frequently appeared whenever the boulder was mentioned.[129] The comparison became so overused as to become cliché and irritating to those who heard it. On one of the visiting cards traditionally left at the site by tourists in the mid- and late 1800s, one had written, "Does not this bowlder remind you of the sword of Damocles?" To this over-

Left: Kilburn Brothers. *Flume above the Boulder*, albumen silver print stereograph, circa 1867. *Courtesy of the Boston Public Library.*

Opposite: W. Hamilton Gibson. *The Flume, Franconia Notch*, in Samuel Adams Drake, *In the Heart of the White Mountains*, 1882. *Author's collection.*

asked question, a *Harper's* reporter finding the card flippantly retorted, "To a civil question, civil reply: No; to me it looks like a nut in a cracker."[130] Benjamin Brown French used a different allusion and likened the boulder to "Mahomet's coffin suspended between earth & heaven."[131]

Others saw the boulder as a metaphor. Minister turned geologist J. Peter Lesley associated it with memory, writing in a letter to his daughter Margaret dated June 13, 1887: "No one can tell just what he will and will not be able to retain in mind. Passing events of the most impressive character slip into oblivion—accidental details of no moment catch in cracks of the brain and stick there to all time, like the boulder in the Flume of the White Mountains."[132]

For years, the boulder received nearly as much attention as the Flume itself and figured in engravings, paintings, daguerreotypes and other visual images that became popular souvenirs as well as marketing tools that spread the notoriety of the Flume. By the 1870s, the boulder had assumed such a firm place in American popular culture that nearly every well-read individual was thought to be familiar with it. One travel writer, when witnessing similar sites in Europe, simply likened them to "the well-known boulder at the Flume,

The Flume Gorge at Franconia Notch

in the Franconia Mountains."[133] Some, like A.E. DeWolfe, then a waiter at the Flume House and later a newspaperman, contended that the boulder was "really a more famous feature of the Notch than the Old Man of the Mountain."[134] Essayist and novelist Charles Dudley Warner, commenting in 1886, maintained that "everyone went there to see a bowlder which hung suspended over the stream in the narrow cañon. This curiosity attracted annually thousands of people, who apparently cared more for this toy than for anything else in the region."[135]

Complementing the boulder as a noted landmark was a fallen pine or hemlock tree, the trunk of which bridged the chasm above the boulder, "suspended high in the air for adventurous visitors. The passage, however, is dangerous, even for those accustomed to such feats."[136] The tree was noted as early as 1841 by Nathaniel Peabody Rogers and by numerous subsequent visitors.[137] While some perceived a step out onto the tree trunk a perilous if not foolhardy adventure, others saw it, and the Flume, more darkly. "It needs a very sure foot and steady head to stand on the insecure bridge, guiltless of a support for the hand, and gaze down into the yawning depths below, and indeed, to one blessed or cursed with a sense of the eternal fitness of things, the temptations to suicide in this dramatic nook are well nigh irresistible."[138] French dissuaded an audacious member of his 1845 party from venturing out onto the tree. "I urged, as a reason why he should not, that he might fall off, & it would be such a trouble to pick him up & carry him home that he had better not run the risk, & either my argument, or *something* else determined him not to perform the feat."[139] One who did tempt fate and almost came to the disaster envisioned by French was William B. Swett, who, while working on the crew repairing the Flume's boardwalks in 1865, tripped when crossing and nearly plummeted into the Flume below. Only a desperate grab onto a bush saved him.[140]

THE UPPER FLUME

Many early tourists failed to venture beyond the suspended boulder. One who did was a fellow abolitionist who accompanied Nathaniel Peabody Rogers there in August 1841.

> *Brother Beach had entered the Flume ahead of the rest of us, and when we had advanced a little way into it, we discovered him, beyond the accessible*

> *path, clambering by the hands along the side of the great wall. He had doffed his hat, coat and waistcoat, and boots and stockings, and was adventuring for the upper end of the cavern. We feared he would "catch his death of cold"—if he did not get dashed to pieces—for it was as cold and damp as a dungeon. We shouted to him at the top of our voice; but he could not hear us, for the roar of the cataract and the distance. He soon disappeared at the bend of the Flume, and we saw no more of him, till a cry overhead made us look up, and we beheld him midway of the bridge.*[141]

As late as 1869, the Flume's wooden walkways still extended only as far as the hanging boulder, and those choosing to investigate the Flume further did so by clambering over rocks and fallen trees. On Frederika Bremer's 1850 visit, she caught a tantalizing glimpse of the gorge above the boulder where she "saw up aloft the stream hurl itself from the left hand into the mountain chasm, in a strong stream, clear as crystal."[142]

Bremer did not explore beyond the boulder largely because hiking to the top of the Flume was generally not considered appropriate for women. Author Jacob S. Trux, writing in the influential literary magazine *The Knickerbocker* in August 1854, recalled a trip to the Flume a decade earlier, when "it was hard work in those days, climbing along those rugged and precipitous paths, and females needed constant and unremitting attention. I presume it is so in some degree still."[143] While the sexism of

Cascades above the Flume, albumen silver print stereograph, circa 1870. *Courtesy of the Miriam and Ira D. Wallach Division of Art, Print and Photographs: Photography Collection, New York Public Library.*

C.P. Hibbard. *Cascade in the Flume*, albumen silver print stereograph, circa 1875. *Courtesy of the Miriam and Ira D. Wallach Division of Art, Print and Photographs: Photography Collection, New York Public Library.*

the commentary was typical of the period, women *did* venture through the entire Flume, at times leaving their male companions behind. One anonymous visitor in August 1861 recorded her "irresistible desire" to walk up Table Rock and her passage through the Flume, despite being encumbered by skirts. "To run, and jump, and climb were no feats. And I did go, on and on, farther, even, than most of the gentlemen. Had I been dressed like them, I had not stopped where they did. Alas, for the foolish fashions of the times! Hoops and long skirts are an abomination, at the mountains,—to say the least of them.—When next I go they shall be eschewed."[144] A tourist visiting in summer 1878 had a more modest solution than foregoing skirts and informed the *White Mountain Echo* that "the path needs to be extended beyond the boulder, as now beautiful falls and other scenery above it are lost to the visitor, and the only substitute is photographs of the same."[145]

Visitors, and particularly ladies, who completed the journey through the Flume were accustomed to leave a token at the top marking their effort, most often a calling or visiting card, though on one occasion a toad wrapped in a handkerchief was discovered.[146] These items were left lying on boulders and pinned to trees.[147]

THE POOL

Located close by and nearly always coupled with the Flume as an attraction worthy of visiting was the Pool, a deep basin on the Pemigewasset River, which Lanman described as "the most superb pool in this whole country."[148] Its location indicated by a simple roadside sign near the Flume House stable, the Pool was approached by a footpath described in 1853 as "uneven, crooked and narrow" but still pleasant. As late as the end of the century, this way remained unimproved, "a path through damp woods that smell of fern and toadstools, and over slippery fallen logs for a half mile or more."[149] Planks were placed across wet and miry patches of ground, making it of easier access, "especially for ladies."[150] All agreed that "the half-mile walk is full of variety and very improving—to the appetite."[151]

Though the Pool path passed through pleasant woodland and was studded with moss-covered boulders, there was no "premonitory view" of the Pool. The visitor simply came upon it, finding "himself on the brink of a precipice falling with a sheer descent one hundred and fifty feet to the surface of the agitated waters below."[152]

Like the Flume, the Pool was the result of geological forces when between fourteen thousand and twenty-five thousand years ago a silt-filled rivulet began to flow from the glacier and abrade the surrounding rock. For many

E. & H.T. Anthony. *The Pool*, albumen silver print stereograph, circa 1860. *Courtesy of the Miriam and Ira D. Wallach Division of Art, Print and Photographs: Photography Collection, New York Public Library.*

years, the depth of the Pool was grossly exaggerated. Starr King described it as 150 feet broad and nearly as deep, although its depth has since been ascertained as being only about 40 feet. The walls that nearly completely enclose it reach a height of 130 feet.[153] The Pool's waters historically were referred to as black, inky, dark green and "lustrous sea-green."[154]

Surrounded by towering pines that only infrequently let in the sun, the Pool was frequently noted for its melancholy aspect.[155] "Gloomy," "weird," "black," "frowning," "somber," "rank," "silent," "opaque," "dreary" and "morbid" were words that continually were employed to convey a sense of the site's perceived bleakness.[156] One writer later described the Pool as "lying under the shadow of darkling cliffs like a monster in wait for its prey."[157] Analogies were frequently drawn from ancient Greece, and the Pool was compared to the mythological river of the dead, the river Styx. "It is said to look Stygian, and all that by daylight, and was certainly a sombre [*sic*] looking hole in the dusk of evening."[158] For many, the stillness and quietude of the Pool with its towering cliffs "alone were worth the whole trouble and expense of a visit to the mountains."[159]

Visitors could either stand and overlook the Pool or descend a steep staircase some seventy-five to one hundred feet to its lip, from where they could better admire the small cascade of the Pemigewasset. The spray of this

The Leighton & Valentine Co. *The Pool and Stairs, Franconia Notch, White Mountains, N.H.*, lithographic postcard, circa 1905. *Author's collection.*

small fall was touted to have "heeling" properties, or so noted a misspelled sign seen by members of the Yale Glee Club in 1861.[160] Some visitors in their eagerness to view the Pool approached too close, with disastrous results. The Pool was the site of one potentially serious mishap when, in August 1852, Lothrop Smith of New Orleans

> *made a misstep over the precipice near the Flume House into the abyss below. He fell into the pool, from which, by great presence of mind, though the water was icy cold, and he was incumbered* [sic] *with his clothes, he made his escape by swimming to a crag of the rock on a level with the water. Here, we are told, he was lodged about forty feet beneath the distance from which he fell. There was no means of ascent except by ropes, which were procured by friends who were with him at the time of the fall. He fastened a rope round his body and was raised aloft, drenched and bruised, but the only human thing, we presume, that ever came from the pool alive after such a fall.*[161]

In September 1895, George R. Porter, while on a long-distance bicycling touring trip with the Massachusetts Bicycle Club, fell into the pool with his camera. Both he and the camera were retrieved. Reportedly, neither was injured.[162]

THE PHILOSOPHER OF THE POOL

Long associated with the Pool was John Merrill (1802–1892), known to tourists as the "Philosopher of the Pool." Merrill remained a fixture there each summer for thirty-four years, during which time he sold refreshments and souvenirs and paddled tourists about for a fee while expounding upon his favorite philosophical themes.

A native of Bristol, New Hampshire, Merrill came to view the Pool in 1853 and immediately conceived the idea of taking tourists onto its waters. He later explained to one reporter:

> *The day I first came here, there was a party of at least forty in number, standing over there on that rock and around it* [nearly opposite the fall]. *They were awful anxious to get close to the fall there, and I thought I could manage to get them there with a little trouble. So up I clambered until I*

> *reached the top of the rocks there, and then I turned to and built a boat; it wasn't much of one, to be sure, but it answered the purpose, and then I manufactured a rope and let her down the side of the cliff there into the Pool. You may be sure they enjoyed the row.*[163]

Merrill paid the Flume House seventy-five dollars annually for the concession. To make money, Merrill took guests from April through September onto a large flat-bottomed barge fitted with carpet-covered seats along the sides and removable benches across the center and pulled them by means of paddle and a rope. Along with his wife, Rhoda, Merrill also sold pictures and books. Percy Curtiss mentions that Merrill provided refreshment, a "concoction which the old man offered at ten cents per glass, under the title of lemonade."[164] Other visitors found the lemonade very good and noted that maple sugar, a New Hampshire vacation staple, was also available.[165] Numerous stereographic cards showing the Pool were sold as well, many of which Merrill obliged the purchaser by autographing on the back.[166]

Each summer Merrill resided at the Pool, and he claimed that since having done so he had never had a cold.[167] While not busy attending to visitors, he is believed to have constructed a path linking the Pool and the Flume.[168] In 1867, he relocated to Pardeeville, Wisconsin, but continued to return each summer to the Pool.

What set Merrill apart as unforgettable and earned for him a place in White Mountains lore were his philosophical views on cosmogony, the study of the origins and evolution of the universe, which he readily shared with visitors. Introducing himself to visitors as Professor Merrill, he propounded his theory "that this earth is not a solid sphere, but a hollow world, more flattened at the extremities than is usually admitted; that it is open at the northern and southern extremities admitting heat, light, air and space inside; that there are continents and oceans within as habitable and navigable as those on the outside."[169] He advanced his belief that famed Arctic explorer Sir John Franklin, who had disappeared in 1845, was in fact inside the Earth, having entered through a polar opening.

To illustrate his talk, Merrill had symbols resembling bull's eyes painted on one of the Pool walls. "On the side of the rock opposite his boats," reported one visitor in 1865, Merrill "has drawn some diagrams which are enveloped in mysterious letters and figures,…and if you ask him what they mean, he will propose to row you over for a quarter of a dollar, and explain to you the whole thing, and when he has done so you will know just as much about it

Right: John P. Soule. *The Philosopher of the Pool* [John Merrill], albumen silver print stereograph, circa 1860. *Courtesy of the Miriam and Ira D. Wallach Division of Art, Print and Photographs: Photography Collection, New York Public Library.*

Below: Kilburn Brothers. *The Pool, Franconia Notch*, albumen silver print stereograph, circa 1867. *Author's collection.*

F.G. Weller. *The Pool*, albumen silver print stereograph, circa 1870. *Courtesy of the Miriam and Ira D. Wallach Division of Art, Print and Photographs: Photography Collection, New York Public Library.*

as you did before, and probably just as much as he does."[170] The concentric circles were in fact intended to represent polar and equatorial cross-sections illustrating Merrill's hollow-earth view that the globe was composed of various layers—cloud, earth and ocean.

Merrill also lectured on cosmogony in the parlor of the Flume House, publishing a copy of his address in 1858.[171] Fortunately, a firsthand account of Merrill's Flume House lecture exists. Commencing at "early candle-light," Merrill displayed complimentary letters from Queen Victoria and others that were later revealed to have been a hoax perpetrated on Merrill, though he believed in their authenticity. "The lecture that followed was an odd compound of geology run mad and grammar bewitched," observed one listener. Merrill concluded by distributing a circular outlining his plan for poor relief.[172]

In keeping with the mythological analogies commonly used to describe the Flume and the Pool in the mid-1800s, many visitors drew upon ancient Greece in their search for a fitting description for Merrill. *Harper's* remarked that the stranger might be excused if they were to confuse Merrill with the "ferryman of Hades."[173] Others similarly saw Merrill as "grim and silent as Charon [as] he paddles his clumsy old boat around the pool, the company on board sitting dumb as a group of condemned souls crossing the Styx, while the black water splashes around them, and the spray from the sullen cascade dashes against their faces."[174]

Merrill was alternately characterized as a crank, a cheat and a fool. One critic, alluding to Merrill, described the Pool as "much of a joke and something of a reality."[175] Starr King failed to mention Merrill in his 1859 guidebook, doubtless due to their likely theological differences. Two of the "Pemigewasset Perambulators," a party of eleven hikers who visited in July 1866, deemed Merrill "a swindler, and would not take a ride in his big square, boat." The remainder each paid Merrill fifteen cents for the pleasure of doing so and listened to Merrill's theories. Sophia Thoreau, visiting in 1870, recorded her impression that Merrill "had gone crazy on cosmogony."[176]

Some were likely put off by Merrill's presence, including possibly the *New York Herald*, which in 1869 termed the Pool hardly worth a visit.[177] Some, however, argued that the eccentric Merrill was in fact one of the attractions of the place.[178] Still others were, fortunately, more kind. Kinsman Samuel Merrill in his Merrill family genealogy published in the early twentieth century recalled, "I met him there [at the Pool] one day in the early '70s of the last century. He impressed me as a kindly old man, who could talk entertainingly and intelligently on many subjects."[179] Members of the Yale Glee Club visiting in 1861 found him irresistible.[180]

Despite the fact that, as one commentator recorded, "he gives the impression of a dreamy visionary, too unpractical to make his way amongst his fellow-men in the rude jostle of life[,…] he is no fool. He comes here

Littleton View Company. *Pool, Franconia Notch, N.H.*, albumen silver print stereograph, circa 1870. *Courtesy of the Miriam and Ira D. Wallach Division of Art, Print and Photographs: Photography Collection, New York Public Library.*

from the West, has summered here twelve years, and in that time has saved enough from acting as cicerone at the Pool to buy two large farms."[181] Merrill, who increased his boat fee to a quarter in the 1870s, was reported by one newspaper in 1874 as earning $700 to $800 annually from visitors, while his notoriety and receipts continued to climb, reaching $1,500 in summer 1886.[182] Henrietta Payne-Westbrook estimated his net worth in the late 1880s shortly before he retired as $12,000.[183] "Charity says he is a crack-brain, but we fancied there was a method in his madness that betrayed the Yankee trick."[184]

In 1888, Merrill left the Pool for good and returned to his Wisconsin homestead to live out his days. At the time, he submitted the following touching letter to the *White Mountain Echo* for publication.

> *Mr. Editor: Please say to my friends that I have retired from The Pool, after being there 34 years, and concluded to spend the rest of my days on the homestead in Pardeeville, Wis. where I can sit and see the 100 acres of crops almost ready for harvest. Crops never looked better. Give my best and respects to all, till we meet in heaven. I am almost home. This is my eighty-seventh year. Am well, only old age says stay with my children. Yours in love,*
>
> *JOHN MERRILL*

CHAPTER 4

"THE SENSELESS RIOTING OF MAN"

THE INFLUX BEGINS, 1850–1861

THE CROWDS

By the mid-1850s, the Flume had become a "national symbol of the wonders of natural beauty" and, as such, a mandatory stop on any White Mountains itinerary.[185] Newspaper travelogues brought the popular attraction to the attention of readers throughout the nation, and many deemed the Flume the principal sight to be viewed in the region.[186] In an era when marketing was limited, the owners of the Flume House were fortunate in the word-of-mouth advertising that widely spread awareness of their attraction. Souvenir stereoscopic card images also helped. The result was a flood of tourists who began to arrive at mid-century.

Intellectuals who sought a more contemplative experience at the Flume were disappointed not always to find it there, largely due to the crowds, which were composed of guests not only of the Flume House but those of other hotels who had made the trek to visit the Flume. "Wagons are constantly taking parties from the Profile House" to see the Flume, Pool and Basin, reported one visitor in 1855.[187] The spacious Profile House wagons, driven in the 1860s by Ed Cox, were capable of transporting fifteen and were said to have good springs, an important criteria given the rocky road that led through the notch to the Flume.[188] By 1886, these were running at regularly scheduled times and included stops at not only the Flume and Pool but the Basin as well.[189] So interesting

Henry S. Fifield. *Visitors at the Flume*, albumen silver print stereograph, 1871. *Courtesy of the Miriam and Ira D. Wallach Division of Art, Print and Photographs: Photography Collection, New York Public Library.*

were the occupants of these conveyances that they themselves became an attraction, at least for journalist and travel writer W.C. Prime, who watched them passing on their way to the Flume from a shaded spot near the road.[190]

Hawthorne's aversion to tourists elsewhere in the White Mountains is relatively well known, but Swedish author Frederika Bremer was similarly put off by the White Mountain crowds, which seemed more intent on socializing than regarding the landscape. Bremer complained of the "noisy, unquiet company, who do not seem to understand any other mode of enjoying nature than in talking, laughing, eating, drinking, and by all other kinds of noisy pleasures….How unlike is this thoughtless life to that of nature, where the clouds come down as if to converse with the mountain….The senseless rioting of man in the midst of this grandeur of nature makes me almost sad for my kindred."[191] By 1859, Starr King noted that crowds at the Flume had become so large and frequent that they diminished visitors' enjoyment of the feature. He recorded that "most persons see it only once, and then in connection with large parties when there is too much confusion, distraction, and chatter."

Johan Gustaf Sandberg. *Fredrika Bremer*, oil on wood, 1843. *Courtesy of Nationalmuseet, Stockholm.*

In order to avoid these crowds, Starr King recommended staying at the Flume House and visiting the Flume in early morning either alone or in the company of but a very small party. "The beauty of the place will open itself as it cannot in the first visit, and as it will not to a crowd."[192] Guidebook publisher George L. Keyes in 1874 similarly recommended a morning visit before breakfast as "a grand experience and good appetizer," while half a century on, Flume reservation director C.T. Bodwell continued to maintain that morning was the best time to view the Flume.[193] Starr King also implicitly recommended multiple visits to the Flume, and a correspondent for the *Boston Daily Atlas* in 1852 would have agreed, insisting that "the flume, cascade and pool, deserve more than a single visit."[194]

PAINTERS, POETS AND NATURALISTS

In the mid-nineteenth century, art and poetry helped celebrate and popularize the Flume for many Americans, while science sought to explore and document its wonders up close. The thoughts and images that they produced not only became part of the American literary, artistic and scientific canon but also helped usher in the era of scenic tourism. Richard Taft reprinted remarks by both Bremer and Starr King as endorsements of Franconia Notch's scenery in his advertisements, successfully encouraging tourists to stay in his hotels.[195]

The *New York Times* considered southern Franconia Notch, the Flume and the Pool as "a very Paradise for the landscape sketcher" and recognized the Flume House as a favorite summer resort for landscape painters.[196] Daniel Huntington agreed, calling Franconia Notch "a very agreeable and desirable place for landscape study."[197] Many artists, both amateur and professional, made the journey to the notch in search of subjects, especially once they perceived the art colony at North Conway as overrun by their colleagues. Once there, they produced works in the style of the Hudson River School, which celebrated the grace and beauty of uniquely American scenery. In August 1859, one party made several visits to the Flume and was pleased to come away with a number of sketches, despite the low water running in Flume Brook.[198] Many artists, like Josiah Wolcott, came "to get more knowledge of the natural scenery." "I have not been idle, but have stored my mind with much valuable material for future use," Wolcott later wrote. "Every cloud, hill, tree, bush, running stream, or other natural object, seems to have a charm which I did not see before. An increased store of sketches can testify to that."[199]

In 1857, the art journal *The Crayon* reported that Sylvester Phelps Hodgdon, a student of Benjamin Champney and "one of our most promising painters," had completed a landscape of the Pemigewasset valley viewed from the Flume House, a scene he treated again in 1872.[200] Franconia Notch was a favored locale for Hodgdon, who as a lithographer for L.H. Bradford in Boston in the early 1850s was responsible for the execution of a number of views of Franconia Notch, including one of the Flume.

John Badger Bachelder also produced images of the area, including a small watercolor depicting tourists climbing through the Flume. The Flume and its iconic boulder were irresistible subjects for many artists, including Wolcott (*The Flume*), John Frederick Kensett (*The Flume with Boulder*), Thomas Hill (*The Flume with Boulder*) and Samuel Lancaster Gerry, who produced two paintings (*The Flume with Boulder* and *The Flume*, which may have been a preliminary study for the first) depicting a lone figure trekking through the gorge.

One of the most frequently mentioned Flume paintings was *The Boulder and the Flume* (1878) by self-taught artist Ralph A. Blakelock. Blakelock's painting depicts the Flume as a gloom-shrouded chasm with dense vegetation. The narrowness of the Flume and the verticality of its walls are accentuated by Blakelock, creating a claustrophobic feeling for the viewer. Some have cited the painting as a reflection of the emotional and financial stresses that Blakelock contended with throughout much of his life, as well as a product of his need to earn a living.[201] Robert L. McGrath supports this contention, writing that "paying lip service to the symbolism of the landscape as a meditation on the pilgrimage of life, Blakelock was probably less concerned with spiritual transcendence than with creating a marketable product for the tourist trade."[202] Edward Hill's *The Flume*, painted following the loss of the suspended boulder, is similarly criticized by McGrath as devoid of "transcendent meanings" and representative solely of "the mundane actualities of place rather than the spiritual ideals

Edward Hill. *The Flume*, oil on canvas, late nineteenth century. *Private collection.*

of redemption, salvation, or moral elevation."[203] Both depictions were merely reflective of the waning influence of the sublime as commitment to a personal artistic aesthetic for some artists gave way to the more commercialized images demanded by tourists.

The nearby Pool received similar attention from artists. A. Zeno Shindler, later noted for his ethnographical portraits and photographs of Native Americans, treated the subject in his 1859 painting *The Pool, Franconia Mountains, N.H.* The Pool was also painted by Thomas Hill in his simply named *The Pool* (circa 1875), which depicts a tourist couple being poled from shore by John Merrill, as well as in a second painting, *Fishing in Merrill's Pool.*

Many of the images these artists produced were published as engravings in the journals of the day, helping bring the Flume and Pool to the attention of a wider audience. Among the most proficient of the engravers and chromolithographers who treated the Flume was J.H. Bufford of Boston, who produced a series of twenty-four lithographs depicting White Mountain scenes, including the Flume and the Pool, published as *Bufford's Colored Views of the White Mountains and the Vicinity* in 1863.

Besides contributing visually to an American understanding of wilderness in the mid-nineteenth century, the Flume inspired both the public and private writings of nineteenth-century poets and authors who celebrated nature. New Hampshire poet-politician Harry Hibbard was one of the first to poeticize the Flume in his lengthy "Franconia Mountain Notch," written at the age of twenty and first published in the *Democratic Review* in April 1839. The poem contains a stanza devoted to the sublimity of the Flume that was frequently included in nineteenth-century poetry anthologies:

And farther down from Garnsey's lone abode,
By a rude footpath climb the mountain side,
Leaving below the traveller's winding road,
To where the cleft hill yawns abrupt and wide,
As though some earthquake did its mass divide
In olden time; there view the rocky Flume,
Tremendous chasm; rising side by side,
The rocks abrupt wall in the long high room,
Echoing the wild stream's roar, and dark with vapory gloom.[204]

Emerson, who extolled the ministering power of nature and laid the foundation of Transcendental philosophy in his powerful 1836 essay "Nature," visited the Flume in 1839 and later confided in his journal

Right: Ralph Albert Blakelock. *The Boulder and the Flume*, oil on canvas, 1883. *Courtesy of the Metropolitan Museum of Art.*

Below: Thomas Hill. *The Pool [Merrill's Pool]*, oil on mounted paper, circa 1875. *Private collection.*

that "I long sometimes to have mountains, ravines and flumes like that in Lincoln, New Hampshire, within reach of my eyes and feet."[205] For Emerson, the Flume was suffused with the divine. He nonetheless grew unfamiliar with the chasm over time, not recollecting it when he again visited in the company of his daughter Ellen in June 1875. Setting out nearly immediately upon their arrival at the Flume House, Ellen recorded that "a sudden oblivion had removed from Father's memory his former visit here. He wondered at my wayward folly in setting forth without asking questions. How did I know how far it might be, which way to go, indeed what was it we were going to see? 'What is the Flume?' he asked. 'Is it a mountain or a river, or a tree, or a rock!'" Upon seeing the Flume once more, "he said he remembered having admired something long ago, and this was it, and worthy!"[206]

Reflecting the movement away from early nineteenth-century Romanticism and Emersonian Transcendentalism, many younger poets and writers began to depict the Flume as a place of beauty rather than sublimity or divinity. Lucy Larcom mentioned the Flume in her August 1867 poem "My Mountain" and four months later simply wrote that she had never seen "anything lovelier than the green light with which the grotto is flooded by the afternoon sun."[207]

The Flume also attracted scientists and naturalists curious to explore the natural world. Clergyman turned geologist J. Peter Lesley visited the White Mountains, including the Flume, as early as 1849. Probably Lesley was the person described in the 1862 tale *The White Hills in October* as "a fine, intelligent, genteel-looking person, who proved to be a clergyman whom [the protagonist] Alice had once before met at the Flume-House. He is a true lover of nature and explorer of nature's secrets, a geologist, botanist, etc. etc. and he most wisely comes up to the high places at all seasons, whenever he feels the need of refreshment to his bodily and mind's eye."[208]

The Flume had its appeal for ornithologists as well as botanists, particularly those interested in the mosses, lichens, ferns and algae that throve on the gorge's temperate acidic walls and wet seepage.[209] Emerson noted the abundance of these plants, their profusion a delight to his companion, Mr. Bradford, who "found this wild place the Gretna Green of Botany, for it was the den of all cryptogamous [seedless] plants."[210] Amateur botanist Elizabeth Hoar visited in August 1852 and returned to Concord, Massachusetts, where she showed Thoreau lichens, mosses and convallaria berries she had gathered.

H.C. White Co. *Looking down the Rocky Gorge of the Flume, Franconia Notch, White Mts., N.H., U.S.A.*, albumen silver print stereograph, 1909. *Courtesy of the Library of Congress.*

The Flume was considered an ideal habitat for algae given that the walls were nearly constantly covered in moisture and remained unexposed to direct sunlight. "Nearly everywhere the wall is covered with a dark reddish brown coating; specimens of this taken at different points showed that it was practically the same throughout, four species of algae being found in all the specimens, though varying in relative abundance."[211] William Gilson Farlow, professor of cryptogamic botany at Harvard, visited in the early 1880s and reported five species of algae present at the Flume.[212]

PHOTOGRAPHS AND SOUVENIRS

While artistic, literary and scientific works well documented the wonders of the Flume, these generally were viewable by only a limited audience, and it was not until the refinement of photography coupled with developments in the field of printing that mass-produced images of the Flume became widely available to the public. Once they did, they quickly replaced paintings, drawings and engravings as more realistic and reliable reminders of place.

Prior to the advent of picture postcards in the very late nineteenth century, the most popular Flume souvenirs were stereoscopic views, two nearly identical images pasted onto sturdy oblong cards that created a three-dimensional image when viewed through a stereoscope. Photographers took numerous images of the Flume, the Pool, the Flume House and surrounding attractions for use by stereoscopic card manufacturers, including Kilburn Brothers and G.H. Aldrich and Company of Littleton, Nathan W. Pease of North Conway and John P. Soule of Boston. The resultant cards were marketed to tourists hungry for souvenirs.

Photographers also produced cabinet cards, larger photographs mounted onto thick decorative cardboard backings available in a range of sizes, with various views of the Flume and Pool. The Flume was also the subject of magic lantern slides and stereopticons, forerunners of slide projectors, which broadcast images onto a wall or sheet for public presentations. Thomas Hall in Boston, established in 1835, and the Soule Photograph Company, also of Boston, were noted producers of Flume-related glass slides.[213]

For photographers like F.B. Gage who captured images of the Flume, the process was often difficult. Gage documented his efforts to photograph the Flume for E. & H.T. Anthony in the late 1850s, which involved hauling his apparatus, including a cumbersome C[harles] C. Harrison stereoscopic camera and tent, into the Flume. On the first day, Gage found the sky overcast, and it was impossible to take images due to the lack of light. Three days later, bright sunshine encouraged Gage to renew his efforts.

> *In a short time our tent was raised, and we prepared and exposed a plate with the full aperture; we exposed it three minutes, and on development it proved much under-exposed. Another trial of six minutes proved it to be the right exposure and developed a fine negative. This exposure of six minutes was 120 times longer than we would have exposed in the open country, from which you can imagine the depth and gloom of the place.*[214]

The Flume, Franconia Range, showing Henry S. Fifield's studio, from *Harper's New Monthly Magazine*, August 1877. *Author's collection.*

More personalized views could be had at the Flume Picture Gallery from photographer Henry S. Fifield (circa 1822–1881) of New Hampton, New Hampshire. Beginning about 1861, Fifield took up seasonal residence at the Flume House and conducted a portable studio between July 1 and early October each summer in the Flume. Fifield advertised himself as an artist, though he was typically described as "an enterprising photographist on the spot [who] avails himself of the opportunity when there are a large number of visitors, to take photographs for which he finds a ready market for future delivery at remunerative prices."[215] Fifield also retailed souvenir photographs and stereoscopic cards, an operation mentioned by author Percy Curtiss, who left his characters "Mrs. Coburn and Mrs. Freelingheit selecting photographic views at the little photograph saloon half-way up the Flume."[216]

Fifield's small Flume studio was described in 1865 as a "picture gallery." "Though the gallery is mostly out of doors, the little shanty at which my letter is dated [is] used as a sort of laboratory or workshop by the Artist, who furnishes a good stereoscopic view of the Flume with the purchaser in it, for the moderate sum of one dollar."[217] Visitors from Indiana similarly described the operation twelve years later in 1877:

> *Away up here, just below this natural curiosity* [the suspended boulder], *is a rude shanty where a deformed man takes stereoscopic views and derives a profitable income from this trade, for how few there are who can resist the temptation to have their "pictures took," and soon all of our party save one (who had given out and returned to the hotel to rest) posed with Alpine stocks in their hands, and, had not the wee small boy got up and turned around to see how the others looked, and the next small boy shaking his finger at him, bidding him to sit still, the picture would have been a success.*[218]

Many visitors took advantage of Fifield's services, including a group of eleven campers self-dubbed the Pemigewasset Perambulators who visited in mid-1866. "We were photographed here, and got a very good picture, which we value very much, as it shows just how the eleven Perambulators looked as they frogged it through the mountains."[219] Among the most famous photographed by Fifield was First Lady Mary Todd Lincoln, who visited in 1863 accompanied by a party that included her sons Tad and Robert Todd Lincoln and posed for a group portrait.[220] Many of Fifield's images depict well-dressed tourists like Edward Marshall Messenger, who described

Henry S. Fifield. *Mary Lincoln at the Flume*, albumen silver print stereograph, summer 1863. The first lady was in New England recuperating from a carriage accident. *Lincoln Financial Foundation Collection, courtesy of the Allen County Public Library and Indiana State Museum.*

Henry S. Fifield. *Visitors at the Flume*, albumen silver print stereograph, circa 1870. *Courtesy of the Boston Public Library.*

his own 1871 photograph taken in the company of his traveling companion Clarence Tilden of Keene: "A picture I still possess, which was taken at the Flume, tells the story of 'the boys,' with our natty suits, canes and tall, white kersey hats—we were then up-to-date tourists."[221] The reverse side of Fifield's stereo cards were stamped with particulars and carefully numbered for easy identification. "Stereoscopic or Album Views can be had by any persons who have had Negatives taken in the Flume within the last six years by sending to H.S. Fifield, New Hampton, N.H., any time excepting in July, August and September."[222]

Despite the high price, many took the opportunity to be photographed, and the resultant stereoscopic card became a treasured keepsake. "It is a perfect picture, a credit to the artist," the *Nashua Daily Telegraph* reported of one, "and a souvenir that will doubtless be highly prized by those who were of the party."[223] Numerous Fifield images depicting Victorian-era tourists posing with the boulder suspended in the background not only serve as a reminder of this operation but constitute a rich visual documentary history of the nineteenth-century Flume.[224]

In addition to photographic and stereographic images, nineteenth-century Flume souvenirs included, among other articles, decorative porcelain and china, paperweights, spoons and mauchlineware (Scottish-produced varnished wooden boxes and household items), all depicting images of the Flume.[225] In 1878, at least two souvenir dealers were present, including a

Victorian-era Flume souvenirs included stereoscopic cards, cabinet cards, guidebooks and china like this Wedgwood transferware bowl. *Author's collection.*

young woman who sold pictures and baskets of mosses in order to support her mother.[226] This was likely "Little Elsie," who occupied a rustic shelter below the photographic studio and used her funds for the education of herself and her siblings.[227]

Other souvenir items could be purchased at this small shelter that stood at the end of the carriage road into the Flume just above the Pemigewasset River where horses were left before proceeding on foot and near the present Boulder Cabin. The building was described by Henrietta Payne-Westbrook, who visited in the late 1880s, as a "chalet, a tourist's rest, and a place of sale for alpen-stocks, birch beer and souvenirs."[228] Responsible for the operation of this store as well as one at Echo Lake was Mason D. Dolloff of Lincoln, who combined the occupations of lumberman and souvenir-dealer. About the time Payne-Westbrook visited, Dolloff was in partnership with bothers Darius O. and Isa M. Hanson as Dolloff & Hanson, which firm operated a bobbin and chair stock manufactory as well as the Flume House Café.

THE FLUME IN GUIDEBOOKS

Helping provide more readily available and in-depth information about the Flume and the Pool were the numerous inexpensive guidebooks that appeared at mid-century. Starr King's *The White Hills: Their Legends, Landscape and Poetry* (1859), a mix of literary allusions and practical advice, was responsible for bringing the White Mountains to greater attention and became a bestseller. More consistent with the modern understanding of what a guidebook should be and among the best were Eastman's *The White Mountain Guidebook* (1858), Sweetser's *The White Mountains: A Hand Book for Travellers* (1876) and *Chisholm's White Mountain Guide-Book* (1880), all of which provided the requisite description and details of the Flume and Pool, including their dimensions, origins and a brief history.

Steamship and railroad companies also issued their own guidebooks, advertising not only the Flume but also the means to reach it. The *Portland, White-Mountains & Montreal Rail-road Guide* (1853) made mention of the Flume and Pool, while the Norwich & New London Steamship Company touted its maritime and rail connections that linked New York via Norwich, Connecticut, with the Flume House.[229] Other railroads such as the Boston & Maine advertised the Flume and the Pool in an effort to draw passenger traffic.[230]

Eastern Illustrating and Publishing Co. *The Flume, Franconia Notch, White Mts., N.H.*, circa 1900. *Author's collection.*

Eager to promote visitation, one aspect of the Flume generally left unmentioned by guidebook authors of the period were the black flies of late May and early June, which diminished the pleasure of visitors. The following description, dating from 1874, was an exception:

> *The garden of Eden had its serpent; and the Flume, as well as every other place in the mountains, has its pest in the shape of a mosquito or midge. Our ancestors used to believe that the* [devil] *appeared to them*

> *in various shapes, as a goat, or hare, or black cat; had they lived among the White Mountains, they would have embodied him in a mosquito, or midge, or black fly.*
>
> *It is singular what a small affair will bring you tumbling down from the sublime to the ridiculous. You may be gazing awe-struck upon the wonderful beauties of the Flume; grand and poetic thoughts are coursing through your soul when suddenly, a mosquito settles upon the end of your nose, or a midge insinuate himself into the back of your neck; instantly the sublime and beautiful vanish, the bitten member becomes the centre of sensation, and fruitless assaults upon the offending insect take the place of rapt meditation on the beauties of Nature.*[231]

Pennyroyal, catnip, camphor and other repellents of the period had no power to deter these biting insects, which could only be kept at bay by a smudge of black smoke.

Flies proved an eternal problem not only for guests but for workers at the Flume as well. William B. Swett, while engaged in repair work on the Flume's walkways in 1865, was troubled by black flies. The repair crew built a fire at one end of the Flume and preferred periodically being smoked out over the annoyance of the flies.[232] C.T. Bodwell, director of the Flume Reservation from 1928 through 1947, contended with the dreaded insect, noting in his day book for July 3, 1928, "Flies are bad." Two days later, with no respite in sight, a clearly beleaguered Bodwell noted, "<u>FLIES</u> <u>ARE</u> <u>WORSE</u>." One who has experienced these north woods pests can but sympathize.

CHAPTER 5

"THOSE WHO RUSH FROM THE PROFILE TO THE FLUME"

DOING THE LATE NINETEENTH-CENTURY GORGE, 1861–1900

CLOSURE AND BURNING OF THE FLUME HOUSE

While the Flume attracted an ever-increasing number of visitors throughout the mid-nineteenth century, one action that threatened to undermine this development was the closure of the Flume House, which for a decade had promoted tourism at the gorge. According to the *Philadelphia Inquirer*, the Flume House was shuttered and never fully reoccupied following an 1857 lightning strike that killed two and injured several others when lightning traveled through the building's bell wires.[233] Others claimed that the hotel closed in 1861 when proprietors realized it was more profitable to rent horses to convey tourists to the Flume from the Profile House (which they also owned) rather than providing accommodations at the Flume House.[234] Critics argued that such rampant greed would ultimately destroy Franconia Notch and its attractions. "The fact [is] that the 'Profile house' belongs to a company whose directors are anxious only for heavy dividends…[who] in their grasping will probably ruin the 'Franconia Notch' as a desirable place of resort."[235] Since this time, commercialization of the notch's attractions has remained controversial.

It is also possible that the hotel was closed because it catered to a partially southern clientele. Certainly by the 1861 season, which coincided with the first months of the Civil War, the Flume House had failed to open, and the *Buffalo*

Express noted the following year in August 1862 that the hotel was unoccupied at what otherwise would have been the height of the summer season.[236]

Teetotaling travelers stopping in August 1865 were disgusted to discover that while no accommodations were provided at the vacant hotel, liquor was. "A man lives in the house and keeps a *bar* from which to supply travelers, and more particularly the guests of the Profile House, with brandy and whiskey, but that is all the nourishment or refreshment which the thing affords. We asked for something to eat, but were told that it could not be furnished."[237] The hotel, in fact, appears to have been emptied of furniture by this time. In 1865, when a party of revelers from the Profile House visited, William B. Swett made tables and benches from fence boards to accommodate them.[238]

By 1866, the closure of the Flume House was being commented on nationally. The *New York Times* informed readers in June 1866 that "the Flume House will remain closed, as usual, this and the Profile House being owned by one Company, who find it more profitable to make additions to the latter, and let the former remain unoccupied."[239] Practically abandoned for at least ten years, the Flume House was destroyed by fire in January 1871.

While the closure of the Flume House, which had been so intimately connected with the chasm's development as a tourist attraction, held the prospect of adversely impacting visitation at the Flume, this appears not to have been the case. So well known had the Flume become that visitors were willing to travel a considerable distance from the Profile House and other hotels to gaze upon it, ensuring that it remained among the region's most visited sites.

SECOND FLUME HOUSE

Encouraged by the continuing flow of tourists interested in seeing the Flume and public desire for nearby accommodations, Taft and his partner since 1866, Nathaniel White of Concord, erected a modestly sized replacement hotel on the Flume House site, built in mid-1871 at a cost of $32,000. What is known as the "second" Flume House quickly regained its former popularity, reflecting the middle-class appeal of the earlier hotel. Although it was initially built to accommodate up to seventy-five guests, demand soon exceeded available rooms. "If it were twice as large it could be readily filled," judged one commentator at the start of the 1879 season.[240] And ultimately it was, being enlarged in 1883, when capacity was doubled.

Benjamin W. Kilburn. *The Flume House*, albumen silver print cabinet card, circa 1873. *Author's collection.*

The rebuilt Flume House reestablished its former important association with the Flume, as "nearly all visitors to the Flume and Pool give it a call."[241] Samuel Adams Drake in his *The Heart of the White Mountains* called the hotel "the proper tarrying-place for an investigation of the mountain gorge from which it derives its custom and its name," furthering the connection between the two.[242] Managed by Jacob B. Elliott and later by his sons Seth R. and Josiah R. Elliott, the late Victorian Flume House became noted as a destination for a convivial but refined crowd. "You must know that the Franconia Notch is a place where loud girls are not much favored," reported one western newspaper. "The bad manners of Long Branch and Saratoga [two well-known resorts], are very rarely seen here….A coaching party at the Flume House may be composed of young people who were strangers until two days ago, and who may never meet again; but the average of their deportment is so high that they don't hesitate to make the occasion sociable, and well-bred politeness is seldom broken in upon by gaucheries."[243]

Geared toward the middle class, the Flume House in 1876 was described in one advertisement as: "accommodations very fair, and charges $2 only for supper, lodging and breakfast."[244] Despite these modest rates, the Flume House was profitable. In the mid-1880s, when the tourist trade represented a considerable and still growing business in the White Mountains, the *New York Evening Post* estimated that twenty thousand visitors traveled there

Two Horse-drawn Carriages Full of Passengers at the Flume House, Franconia Notch, N.H., on a Clear Summer Day, glass lantern slide, 1909. *Courtesy of the Appalachian Mountain Club Library & Archives.*

Benjamin W. Kilburn. *Flume House, White Mts.*, following its enlargement, albumen silver print stereograph, circa 1883. *Author's collection.*

each season. Combined, White Mountain hoteliers realized more than $1 million in income, of which $125,000 was taken by the Flume and Profile Houses together.[245] The Flume House, though not as luxurious as the Profile House (the pair would consolidate in 1898 as the Profile and Flume Hotels Company), still maintained considerable cachet for years; in August 1913, First Lady Ellen Axson Wilson would stop there.

A TOLL ROAD

While visits to the Flume since its discovery had been free, in 1871, admission began being charged. In that year, Taft, White, Charles H. Greenleaf and John E. Lyon incorporated as the Lincoln Turnpike Company and were empowered by the New Hampshire legislature to construct and maintain a carriage road from the notch road to the Flume and authorized to collect tolls. The newly formed company was conveyed a right of way over the existing roadway, granted authority to widen the road to three rods (nearly fifty feet) and permitted to acquire sufficient property at the road's terminus near the foot of Table Rock in order to create a roundabout for carriages.[246] The route remained unchanged for years and was described in 1919: "At first the turnpike follows closely beside the main road but soon curves away from it, and then falls abruptly to the romantic covered bridge over the Pemigewasset River. A succession of steep ascents then brings the traveler to a looped end of the road by the rustic souvenir store. Thence to the Flume the climb must be made on foot."[247]

To control access, the roadway was guarded by a tollgate marked by a signboard on which were posted "the rates of toll for man and beast, and the various kinds of vehicles."[248] Tolls were established for pedestrians (two cents); persons on horseback (three cents); each person in a carriage (five cents); horses unattached to a vehicle (two cents); sulkies, chaises or chairs with a horse and two wheels (four cents); pleasure wagons and covered buggies for two persons and four wheels (four cents); coaches, stages and phaetons with two horses and four wheels (six cents); and the same with four horses (eight cents).[249] A tollgate keeper collected payment from visitors, and Henrietta Payne-Westbrook makes mention of one known only as Remus, who was present gathering receipts in the late 1880s.[250] For those circumventing the tollgate, fines amounting to three times the toll were levied.

Franconia Notch Stage Opposite the Flume House, silver print photograph, 1905. Arthur White is the driver of the stage, which is en route to the Profile House. *Courtesy of the Upper Pemigewasset Historical Society.*

The new tolls became a source of criticism, and some visitors long took exception to the fact that a fee was now charged to visit the Flume. As late as 1919, one critic would note the "picturesque opening in the stone wall through which automobiles are forbidden to pass. This is the gateway and place of collection for the Lincoln Turnpike, but barring automobiles seems inconsistent with the public-utility nature of the road."[251]

The rebuilt roadway was carried over the Pemigewasset River by a covered vehicular bridge, though there is considerable disagreement about the history of the bridge itself. According to Franconia historian Sarah Welch, a predecessor to the present Flume Covered Bridge was constructed to carry the carriage road across the Pemigewasset River at the time the turnpike company was formed, and this was likely damaged in the 1883 slide.[252] The current bridge, which some have claimed was used elsewhere and relocated to the Flume where it was needed more, dates from 1886.[253] "It was originally covered with half-inch boards cut in about 30-inch lengths and put on like shingles. These were called shakes

C.T. Bodwell. *Covered Bridge and Mt. Liberty on Bus Road to the Flume Gorge*, real photo postcard, 1933. *Author's collection.*

and served until a new covering was needed to stop leaks. Modern shingles replaced these shakes in 1951."[254]

Since its construction, the bridge has become one of the most iconic images of Franconia Notch, appearing on dozens of souvenirs, products and advertising media. In 1938, Ella Shannon Bowles maintained that "probably no other one of our covered bridges has had more visitors or has been more photographed. Pictures of it have appeared in many periodicals, ranging in variety from the *National Geographic* to a house organ published in the Midwest."[255] Today, its image continues to appear on postcards, calendars and dozens of other items, including promotional brochures such as the 2018 *Covered Bridges and Waterfalls of the White Mountains* distributed for free by White Mountain Attractions.

THE BOULDER SWEPT AWAY

The most dramatic change that occurred at the Flume during the late nineteenth century was one nearly no one foresaw. Many believed the boulder that had been suspended in its precarious position between the walls of the Flume for millennia and that had elicited so much commentary would remain lodged there forever. Starr King described it as "held by a grasp out of which it will not slip for centuries."[256] A writer for *Harper's* likewise maintained that "it must stay where it is until Doomsday, unless released by some passing earthquake."[257] Little could they know that within just years it would be gone, swept away in a devastating landslide on Mount Liberty on July 20, 1883. Harvard geology professor Josiah Dwight Whitney, in a later letter to his brother, lexicographer William Dwight Whitney, would note the irony of the boulder's demise, remarking "that the famous 'boulder,' which had been put up in the Flume by *ice*, according to the glacialists, had been carried away by *water*."[258]

On Monday morning, June 18, 1883, days before the slide, "a fine, misty rain" began falling in the notch and increased the following day. By Wednesday, torrential downpours were accompanied by thunder and lightning. Colonel Charles H. Greenleaf (1841–1924), who had owned the Flume, Flume House, Profile House and other Franconia Notch attractions since the 1881 death of his former partner Richard Taft, in fact recalled four days of drenching rains that saturated the earth and ultimately destabilized the slope. "The Notch was full of moisture, whether fog or clouds we did not know."[259]

Charles H. Greenleaf, from *The Granite Monthly* 21, no. 3 (September 1896). *Author's collection.*

The weather culminated in a terrifying electrical storm on the morning of the twentieth. Summer weather could (and can) be extreme in the notch. William H. Smith, a Boston merchant, and William Blandon of Bethlehem, a hotel clerk, were killed when lightning struck a flagpole on the Flume House on July 18, 1857, and passed through the building.[260] Heavy summer rains that loosened soil could occasion landslides along the steep slopes of the region's mountains, as had been the case with the Willey slide of August 1826 and would also be true for slides in 1885 and later.

One of the Flume House guests, a Mr. Langton, reported watching the electrical storm late on the morning of July 20 from the hotel as lightning played about the summit of Mount Liberty. It is believed that a strike on Mount Liberty coupled with "a fearful body of water resembling a waterspout" produced the subsequent slide, unloosing a violent slurry of stones and boulders, uprooted trees, mud and earth.[261]

Three slides actually occurred during the storm, and "it was one of the lesser slides from the face of Mount Liberty which passed through the Flume, and, dividing into three parts as it neared the river upon which the Flume opens, widened and deepened the gorge of the Flume."[262] This slide traveled nearly four miles downward, scouring a channel estimated as thirty feet deep and from twenty to two hundred feet wide, at one point dividing and leaving the ground in between untouched.[263] "The rocky avalanche after meeting the Flume Brook [which was swollen from days of rain] had turned almost a right angle in order to follow its sinuous course" to the Pemigewasset River, sweeping everything before it.[264] Greenleaf recalled a tremendous noise like that of a loud explosion, while one newspaper reported a low rumbling sound, increasing in volume that lasted for three-quarters of an hour and was heard sixteen miles away in Bethlehem.[265] Unaware of the true cause of the thunderous noise, one Flume House guest wondered, "Why are they rolling the bedsteads around in the chambers overhead?"[266]

An item published in the *Philadelphia Times* on July 22 purported to be an eyewitness account of the event by a man identified solely as Amos (likely Amos C. Elliott, brother of the Flume House proprietor), who was out

E.D. Putnam & Sons. *View of Mount Liberty from Indian Head* showing the 1883 Flume landslide scars, real photo postcard, circa 1925. *Author's collection.*

hunting quail for the hotel. While the reporter evidently found Amos and his Yankee accent an object of humor, the New Hampshireman's testimony conveyed the destructive force of such landslides, as well as his extreme luck in having escaped its path.

> *Well, it began to blow and rain, and when I judged I was nigh on to this flume and found I was about two hundred yards back and above there, there came the worst claps of thunder I ever heard in all my life. It lightened up the hull notch and seemed to be half a dozen streaks all jined in one, an' then the thunder come rollin' and boomed up among the mountains dreadful. I was a-hangin' under a big birch an' let go and laid flat on the grass when I heard another sound. First I thought it was the thunder, but it was a different kind of a noise; a rushin', grindin' shriekin' sound, a-growin' louder an' louder, and all of a minute it come so that I thought the hull mountin was a-comin' down. The ground shook and trembled so that when I started to my feet I couldn't hardly stand up, and the noise was frightful. You'd a thought the world was comin' to an end. I could hear rocks a-rollin' an' grindin', trees a-smashin' an' groanin', the snappin' of big limbs, an' the roar and rush increasin' all the time. Then come another blast, an' I got a glimpse through the trees of a pile o' rocks an' trees a-passin' down I*

> *won't say a hundred feet high an' I won't say less. I saw it was a slide, an' thought the hull mountin was comin' so I turned an' left, an' where I run to I don't know.*[267]

The debris flow swept away the Flume's iconic boulder, sheared portions of solid rock from its walls, stripped trees and felled many others while depositing boulders and rocks along the course of the brook. Among the first to visit the Flume following the storm was Langton, who about noon on the twentieth footed it down the carriage road leading from the hotel. Upon reaching the Pemigewasset, the extent of the destruction was evident. The river was choked with mud and strewn with boulders, a portion of the bridge had been swept away and "rock upon rock had been piled in endless confusion. There was nothing but devastation on every side. A little way up the path, or where it had been, rocks and earth were heaped to the width of a thousand feet. In fact, great trees had been snapped asunder and mowed down like tiny reeds."

Greenleaf made an immediate trip to the Flume as well. It was during his inspection that he discovered that the iconic suspended boulder had been swept away. Both Greenleaf and Langton surmised that the boulder had acted as a temporary dam behind which so much debris had accumulated that the resultant pressure forced everything through the Flume, including the boulder. "The loud report was, unquestionably, when the dam gave way, and the boulder went out just the same way that it went in, and was carried several hundred feet down stream."[268]

Though the 1883 Flume slide involved no fatalities, it generated acute national interest, so familiar had many Americans become with the natural wonder. A conjectural picture of the crash of the boulder appeared on the cover of the ever-popular *Harper's Weekly*, conveying the devastating power of the torrential slide, while newspapers as far away as California carried accounts of the event.[269]

In the immediate aftermath of the storm, conflicting reports were made. Some recorded that the boulder had fallen and blocked the Flume while still others that a landslide encompassing one hundred acres had occurred and had filled the Flume completely and destroyed the Flume House.[270] One tourist visiting on August 1 remarked that "the attractive beauty of the Flume disappeared," but newspapers like the *Boston Globe* and *Boston Herald* reported to the contrary that little damage had been sustained and the Flume was "more wonderful than ever" in the aftermath of the disaster, having been lengthened some 505 feet.[271] They pointed to yet another beneficial

Left: W. Hamilton Gibson. *The Fall of the Boulder*, from *Harper's Weekly*, July 14, 1883.

Opposite: W.R.M., Haverhill, Massachusetts. *The Flume above the Bridge, Franconia Notch, White Mts., N.H.* [Avalanche Falls], real photo postcard, circa 1915. *Author's collection.*

consequence of the slide: the formation of what came to be known as Avalanche Falls at the head of the Flume, cascading 45 feet over the red-brown granite ledge.

Given the conflicting reports circulating at the time, visitors in the wake of the slide were uncertain of what to expect. "We had heard it said, 'The Flume is spoiled,' and again, 'It is more wonderful than ever.' Both are true in a measure; before it suggested a miracle, and now it looked as if there had been a 'big freshet.'"[272] Lackluster sentiments such as this may have in fact temporarily reduced visitation. One letter writer to the *Nashua Telegraph*, A.E. DeWolfe, maintained that "the Flume was regarded as about ruined as a 'showplace' and was neglected, all the walks, etc., having been swept away and not replaced."[273] Charles Dudley Warner, however, disputed that there was any decline in the number of visitors. On the contrary, Warner indicated that they arrived "in increasing number, to see where the bowlder once hung."[274]

THE BOULDER LOCATED

In the days that followed, all available workmen were put to work clearing the Flume. "A large number of men with teams were engaged in repairing the roadway and removing the debris that obstructed the approach to the Flume above," noted J.F. Frisbie, who visited on August 1. "The trunks were cut and piled up for removal by team or fire."[275] Additionally, a search for the dislodged boulder was initiated by Greenleaf, who was later reported to have been "very blue" over its loss.[276]

> *I realized we must find the old boulder, which was quickly done.…A gentleman came to me and remarked that this was not the boulder. I replied, "I am satisfied that it is"; but he said, "Why, the old boulder was nearly covered with moss, and in several place tourists had tried to scratch their initials into it." "Yes," said I, "but supposing you had been in that excursion, how much hair would you have had on your head?" He turned away with the smiling rejoinder, "That's the boulder."*[277]

A *Hartford Times* correspondent also identified what he presumed to be the boulder a thousand feet below its former position. While acknowledging that identification of the precise boulder "would seem to have been difficult when so many of similar size and appearance went through the Flume," the reporter felt confident based on its size, the location of smooth surfaces where it had been in contact with the Flume walls and initials that had been cut in various places on its face.[278]

While Greenleaf had no doubts regarding the authenticity of the identified boulder, others did. J.B. Elliott, manager at the Flume House, disputed that the boulder identified by Greenleaf was the boulder in question, while a correspondent of the *New York Evening Post* indicated that the fallen boulder "is now indistinguishable from its neighbors."[279] Some hinted that Greenleaf, as the Flume's owner, was motivated for financial reasons to locate the boulder, or any boulder, and promote it as the famous suspended boulder. "In order to satisfy reasonable human curiosity, the proprietors of the flume have been obliged to select a bowlder and label it as the one that was formerly the shrine of pilgrimage," noted one cynic.[280]

Despite efforts to positively identify the boulder, for most visitors, like one who visited in July 1883, it was inconsequential. "A workman told us he thought he had identified the real boulder farther down amidst the debris; but it matters little for it was not the boulder which was so wonderful, but how it came to be suspended so mysteriously. After seeing the Flume in its present condition, the charm which always clings to mystery is lost, but one is almost overpowered with the thought of the resistless force of Nature's elements."[281] Nonetheless, the loss of the boulder has become such an entrenched part of the Flume's history that its story is told to this day.

VANDALISM

The comments regarding initials carved on the boulder's surface are among the few recorded mentions of nineteenth-century vandalism at the Flume that are known to have been perpetrated. Not only the boulder but also surrounding trees and other natural features were likely targets of less considerate visitors who sought to leave their sad marks on the attraction. At the time of the boulder's fall, the Hartford correspondent took a dim view of the previous defacement of the boulder, remarking that this "is an instance, and possibly the first, where fools' names are seen to advantage in public."[282] These were not the only "fools" at work, for according to Greenleaf, within a week of identifying the fallen boulder, he discovered souvenir hunters had begun chipping away at the rock, necessitating the erection of a low picket fence around it as a barrier.[283]

Another related issue was the unrestricted outdoor advertising that marred the scenery of the region, including the Flume. One particular stereographic card depicting Henry S. Fifield's photographic studio in the middle of the chasm also captured advertising for Drake's Plantation Bitters patent medicine splashed on a rock immediately below.

Patrick H. Drake, manufacturer of the largely rum-based medicine, aggressively advertised the trademark "S-T-1860-X," the obscure meaning of which generated considerable speculation, as Drake intended. Painting smoothly surfaced rocks, stones and trees at White Mountain attractions with the slogan as well as the Plantation Bitters name became an advertising ploy of Drake's, uncaring of the scenic defacement it caused. The prevalence of outdoor advertising painted on rocks, stones and trees in the White Mountains and scenic areas elsewhere like Niagara Falls and the Hudson River, however, ran afoul of public sensibilities. *Harper's Weekly* criticized the practice in an 1865 editorial cartoon by Thomas Nast, and the *New York Tribune* later charged advertisers like Drake with altering "scenery" into "obscenery."[284]

Left: Littleton View Company. *Boulder at Flume, Franconia Notch, N.H.*, albumen silver print stereograph, circa 1883. The suspended boulder is identified and fenced. *Courtesy of the Miriam and Ira D. Wallach Division of Art, Print and Photographs: Photography Collection, New York Public Library.*

Right: Henry S. Fifield. *View of the Flume, Looking Up, Franconia Mts., N.H.*, albumen silver print stereograph, circa 1865. *Courtesy of the J. Paul Getty Museum, Los Angeles.*

As a result of the public outcry that followed Drake's branding of a rock at the base of one of the Mount Washington bridle paths, the New Hampshire legislature in 1864 enacted one of the nation's first laws regulating outdoor advertising to help protect scenic sites like the Flume.[285] While barred from further advertising on natural features, Drake unabashedly used the controversy to further hawk his product in 1865, finding satisfaction in the free advertising the incident had generated:

> *The White Mountains of New-Hampshire are evidently a great institution—very high, heavy frosts, beautiful view, four dollar dinners. But the practical eye of a certain renowned Drake, saw those smooth-faced rocks, and thereupon adorned and variegated the bridle path to the Tip-top House* [on Mount Washington] *with the familiar S.T.—1860—X. PLANTATION BITTERS. This raised the ire of* [opponents] *composing the Legislature of the Granite State, who got their wise heads together, outlawed Dr. Drake, and made it a penal offence to ply the artistic brush on their beloved hills. Verily, the fine arts are at*

a discount in New-Hampshire. Query—Did Drake pay them for this splendid advertisement?[286]

Despite Drake's obvious contempt, the legislative act reflected a growing public demand that New Hampshire's scenic resources like the Flume be protected.

"DOING" THE FLUME

Though the rise of grand hotels in the White Mountains in the second half of the nineteenth century encouraged extended vacations, thousands of excursionists visited for but a few days or at most a week at a time. Quick journeys to view the top attractions became the most common method of touring as early as the 1870s when eager tourists endeavored to visit as many sights in quick succession as possible. Tourists came to appreciate the sheer volume of attractions over quality enjoyment of them, and critics of this method argued that it undermined appreciation of these sights, including the Flume which became the object of many of these tourists' fleeting visits.

The eponymously named hero of the tale "Archie Hutchington," which appeared in *Harper's* in 1871, exemplified this new attitude. Run-down and in need of a restful vacation, Hutchington commits to going to New Hampshire. "I'll go to the White Mountains…Crawford's, Flume, Glen House, Summit House, Tip-top, etc., etc.—I'll do them all, never fear," he breathlessly assures his doctor.[287] Rather than a restful itinerary, Hutchington's plan exemplified the increasing postbellum goal of "doing" the White Mountains. Percy Curtiss similarly made note of "the travelling public,—those who rush from the Profile to the Flume, to the Pool, to Echo Lake, up Mount Lafayette, and through the Franconia region generally in two or three days."[288]

Common on these lists of must-sees was the Flume, which for many became merely another attraction to check off an itinerary. In another story of the period, "The Gibralters: A Story in Four Letters," one of the fictional letter writers, Jack Delano, notes, "My plan had been to leave the stage at the entrance of the Notch, do the Flume and Pool, and follow on to the Profile House later in the day."[289] Increasingly, visitors spoke of "doing" rather than "contemplating." Frances S. Howe of Leominster, who with her companion toured the region in the 1880s by carriage, was one who employed the term. "We are always interested in the excursionists we meet 'doing' the Notch, with its Flume, Pool and basin, for the first time," she confessed.[290] Guidebooks of the era facilitated the practice by providing advice on how best to see these mandatory sights most efficiently. The tourists' appendix included in Samuel Adams Drake's 1882 *The Heart of the White Mountains* advised allotting four hours to visit the Flume and Pool and recommended combining it with a meal at the Flume House.

Newspaper correspondents and letter writers shared their own suggestions "for the benefit of those who for want of time, wish[ed] to 'do' the mountains as quickly as possible."[291] One typical whirlwind excursion in July 1878 departed Concord in the morning and packed in visits to Echo Lake, the Profile, the Basin and the Pool during the afternoon. The following morning, the party departed at 5:00 a.m. to visit the Flume. Passing the toll rate board at the entrance ("which we could not stop to read"), the single-minded group avoided anything of interest that might disrupt their tight schedule and quickly headed for the Flume, where they did not stay long, remarking rather clinically that "ideas [of the Flume] are previously correctly formed from stereoscopic views." Apparently, there was no need to linger viewing a scene that had been so well documented photographically. They were back at the breakfast table at the Flume House by 7:00 a.m.[292]

Package tours that included the Flume became popular during the post–Civil War era. Arranged by private companies, these tours also promoted strictly regimented itineraries consisting of short visits to as wide a range of sites throughout the region as possible. In 1880, the *Nashua Daily Telegraph* advertised a four-day foliage excursion for $3.50.[293] Pierce's weeklong "Special White Mountain Excursion" in early September 1893 from southern New Hampshire cost $15.00, while in 1895 Nason & Durgin of Boston offered for the same fee a "glorious" autumnal tour of the Whites.[294] All included visits to the Flume. Among the most popular tours were those conducted out of Boston by Raymond & Whitcomb. In autumn 1888, the company was conducting eighteen package tours, seven of which included a visit to the Flume.[295] Raymond's tours were designed for the "large number of patrons who find it inconvenient to absent themselves from home or business ties for the time required in the longer excursions, or who desire to make a short tour, occupying only a part of their vacation season."[296] Raymond's also appealed to what it labeled "tourists of a refined and cultivated class," particularly older, novice and lady travelers.[297]

Though such excursions were well conducted and included a variety of sites, the schedule was rigidly adhered to. One package traveler from Bangor,

The Hugh C. Leighton Co. *White Mts., N.H., Flume House*, depicting the Flume House as viewed from the Flume Path, lithographic postcard, circa 1909. *Author's collection.*

Maine, in 1879, while suitably impressed with the convoy of multi-horse teams that conveyed the tour group from the Profile House to the gorge, was dismayed when, upon arrival, the driver announced, "Forty minutes to examine the Flume." Consequently, "all hurried to make the most of their time" despite the fact that "they would like to linger near it for hours."[298] For these tourists, no longer was the Flume to provide an entirely restful or meditative experience.

Among this new breed of tourist visiting the Flume was a large proportion of women. While previously it had been urged that women be escorted by a gentleman when visiting the Flume, one writer marveled at the sheer number

Early twentieth-century women visitors from *Views of the White Mountains with Descriptive Text*, photographic halftone, 1921. *Author's collection.*

Flume House Stable, photographic print from glass negative, late nineteenth century. *Courtesy of the Upper Pemigewasset Historical Society*.

of unaccompanied women he saw there in 1878. "Stage after stage passes loaded inside and out with women, only women. We drive to the Flume, and the cry is, 'Still they come!' We dine at the Flume House…and there they are, 'women to the right of us, women to the left of us.'"[299]

In truth, large numbers of both men and women visited the Flume, and their increasing volume during the post–Civil War era took a physical toll on the site. The *Littleton Courier* recalled in 1924 that during generations past, large numbers of conveyances "from small wagons to the Concord coach" were left at the Flume House stables, indicating the volume of visitors trekking in to see the Flume.[300] By 1878, the tollgate was described as "greatly out of repair," while one visitor in 1879 helpfully suggested regarding the boardwalk that "it would be a good idea to take up the old boards which are getting somewhat rotten and replace them with new plank."[301]

THE FLUME THREATENED

While increasing visitation during the late Victorian era may have caused wear to the Flume's infrastructure, more concerning was the threat posed to the ecological landscape surrounding the Flume by two new developments: railroads and lumbering.

A generation earlier, a railroad through Franconia Notch had been virtually unthinkable, but attitudes changed following the Civil War. In 1868, one Chicagoan traveling by stage remarked "jocosely to the driver that I supposed they would have a horse railway from the Profile to the Flume bye and bye; whereupon he answered that before I am ten years older there will be horse railways all through the mountains with stopping places at every point of interest!" Horrified at the prediction, the midwesterner prodded readers, "If you want any enjoyment in the mountains be sure and come before the railways do."[302] This sense of urgency was not unfounded. In 1878–79, construction of the nine-mile-long Profile & Franconia Notch Railroad between Bethlehem and the Profile House (which one critic labeled as "vandalism") was completed, and within five years, its extension five miles farther to the Flume House was being advocated.[303] While the line would have improved accessibility to the Flume, it would have also diminished the notch's wildness, and it was never built, despite proposals for it being revived in autumn 1895.

Plans for railroads originating at the other end of the notch dated from 1882, when a four-mile extension of the Pemigewasset Valley Railroad was surveyed from its terminus at North Woodstock to the Flume House. Little substantive action was taken until 1895, when overtures were made for a steam railway line to run to a point one mile north of the Flume. While lip service was paid to the fact that the suggested extension would improve tourist access to the gorge, the truer purpose of the line was to open Franconia Notch to lumbering interests.

While limited timbering on the one-hundred-acre lots surrounding the Flume had occurred throughout the mid-nineteenth century, it was not until 1892 that the prospect of deforestation on an industrial scale threatened the Flume.[304] The following year, F.C. Whitehouse of Concord clear-cut a substantial tract on the east bank of the Pemigewasset extending upward toward Franconia Ridge immediately north of the Flume. To process the felled timber and house workers, "unsightly saw-mills and several shanties" were built at present-day Whitehouse Bridge, while milled lumber was carted past the Flume along the notch road due to the lack of any other means of transport.[305] The havoc wreaked upon the region's recreational features by such extensive lumbering was evident in the destruction of the Mount Liberty path above the Flume, which required re-cutting in 1899 by the Appalachian Mountain Club. So devastating was timber-felling near the Flume that fifty acres adjacent to the roadway were purchased as a visual buffer against the unsightly cut-over area.

Throughout the 1890s, various organizations and newspapers such as the *Boston Transcript* and the *Nashua Telegraph* issued strongly worded statements and editorials opposing lumbering in Franconia Notch, citing the possible ecological damage and increased potential for fires that would result.[306] Other critics, however, saw the prospect as a direct threat to the tourist industry, which was increasingly acknowledged as a critical economic catalyst in the region. J.B. Harrison, secretary of the New Hampshire Forestry Commission, maintained that "the culmination of the summer boarding and tourist business is in sight if the destruction of forest conditions in the White Mountains region is allowed to proceed much further unchecked."[307] Historian Francis Parkman, who had known Franconia Notch since his youth, similarly recognized that "blind mismanagement" jeopardized the "abundant income" the region realized through tourism.[308] Some argued that intervention, if not outright state ownership, was necessary to protect tourist revenue. "It is to be regretted that the New Hampshire statute book contains no law to prevent the disfigurement of the beautiful scenes which are the charm of the commonwealth, and attract to it so large an amount of tourist's money," opined the *White Mountain Echo*.[309] Members of the American Forestry Association who visited Franconia Notch in August 1894 were provided an opportunity to visit the Flume, one of the best arguments against logging.

Concerned about the economic and environmental impact of further deforestation on the Merrimack River watershed, the New Hampshire Forestry Commission opposed the 1895 proposals to extend the railroad line from North Woodstock through Franconia Notch. "Such an extension of the Pemigewasset Valley Railroad appeared to this commission to be a project to facilitate and expedite the removal of the forest cover in a portion of the state where every economic reason demanded its preservation, and where denudation already had been carried so far without the aid of railroad facilities as to arouse severest condemnation."[310] Objections from

A View up through a Burned Area between Mount Flume and Mount Liberty, to the Summit of Mount Flume, N.H., on a Partially Cloudy Summer Day, glass lantern slide, circa 1910. *Courtesy of the Appalachian Mountain Club Library & Archives.*

this quarter and elsewhere notwithstanding, the New Hampshire Railroad Commission approved the line, though its mileage was limited to a point below the Flume.

Despite opposition, lumbering at Franconia Notch continued, and by summer 1898, Flume-bound tourists encountered a swath of devastation extending from the Flume entrance to the Basin where the scenery had been destroyed "by the lumberman's axe.…The landscape here is further disfigured by a strip about a quarter of a mile wide, stretching from the river on the right to some distance up the hillside on the left, that was a few years ago covered with handsome trees, but of which nothing now is left but unsightly stumps."[311] About two miles below the Flume, George Johnson began logging around Georgianna Falls and Gordon Pond after acquiring rights there in 1901, establishing the small sawmill-dominated village of Johnson. By 1906, it was estimated that nearly all of the land in the notch had been stripped of its spruce and hardwood except the lands owned by the Profile and Flume Hotels Company.[312] Only with the passage of the Weeks Act in 1911, which authorized the establishment of the White Mountain National Forest, were lands surrounding the Flume protected from this sort of devastation.

CHAPTER 6

"THE EVER-LENGTHENING PROCESSION OF TCHUG-TCHUGGING AUTOMOBILES"

THE MOTORISTS ARRIVE, 1900–1921

AUTOMOBILE TOURING

Improvements to local roadways in the 1890s, when New Hampshire appropriated money for bettering the road between North Woodstock and the Flume, helped pave the way for automobile touring, and by the early 1900s, automobilists began to displace tourists arriving by other means. Both steam and electric street railways countered the threat posed by automobiles by stressing their connections and proximity to the Flume and advertised these in comprehensive guides, hoping to fill their passenger cars with tourists. The Boston & Maine in 1901 emphasized the "rapid transit and luxurious ease" it afforded and the fact that it had largely eliminated the long stage drives previously necessary to reach the Flume.[313] Yet the railroads were unable to compete with the flexibility afforded by the automobile, even after they established supplementary bus routes. No longer were tourists dependent on the schedules of railroads, stages or buses, and as a result, they had much greater freedom in determining their itineraries.

Automobiles made the Flume increasingly accessible, and tourism boomed during the first decades of the twentieth century, promoted by such organizations as the Automobile Club of America. Clearly keeping with the tempo of the times, the *White Mountain Echo* in July 1904 devoted an entire page to the new mode of transport.[314] The following year, the *New York Tribune* featured an article headlined "Motoring a Big Feature of White

W.H. Boardman. *Flume House Stable with Edward W. and Winona (Woodbury) Clement*, silver print cabinet card, August 30, 1909. Clement later served as postmaster at North Woodstock. *Courtesy of the Upper Pemigewasset Historical Society.*

Mountain Summer Life," while its counterpart the *New York Times* reported "Never So Many Motor Parties as Now" in the White Mountains.[315] In July 1913, the Automobile Club of America was charting new scenic routes to and through the White Mountains, including a route from Boston via Plymouth to the Flume.

> *From Plymouth the road is fair gravel to Woodstock. The road is under construction for two miles, but passable. Good gravel is then followed through the Pemigewasset Valley to the Flume. It is a picturesque run. The road runs along a ridge, the Presidential range on the right, high hills on the left, and the river flowing down the centre presenting a charming picture. Many historic points may be visited from* [the] *Flume by leaving the car and walking short distances. Of special interest is the Flume itself, which is a peculiar formation which attracts a large number of White Mountain visitors each year.*[316]

Just one month later in August 1913, the *New York Times* offered New Hampshire–bound motorists advice on "How to Tour for a Week in the Mountains."[317]

The Flume remained a must-see for motorists, and visits were encouraged by several automobile guides that included mention of the

Detroit Publishing Company. *On the Road to the Profile House, Franconia Notch, White Mts., N.H.*, glass negative, circa 1910. *Courtesy of the Library of Congress.*

gorge, including the Green Book, Blue Book and MacNair's Motorway Series.[318] The Flume House specifically targeted automobile tourists, noting in advertising that it opened early in the season and remained open until mid-October in order to accommodate early and late motorists.[319] As a consequence, the number of guests exploded. The *New York Sun* in 1915 claimed the Flume House to be the most visited of the White Mountain hotels, a fact attributable to its connection with the Flume, the hotel making a convenient stop for a meal and souvenirs.[320] The Flume House was recognized as an important rendezvous point for visitors to the Flume, "especially during the noon hours, when crowds of excursionists strike into the Flume."[321]

Though the automobile better suited the new tourists' preference for quick visits to a variety of sites and increased Flume visitation, several commentators disparaged these auto tourists and their superficial taking in of the scenery. The *White Mountain Echo* in 1904 admonished automobilists,

Flume House from *Franconia Notch, White Mountains, N.H.*, photographic halftone, circa 1910. *Author's collection.*

urging them to cultivate "a keener delight in the mysteries of field and wood."[322] Botanist George Golding Kennedy in his journal in September 1915 noted with displeasure "the foolish flying automobile parties" descending upon Franconia Notch.[323] The Appalachian Mountain Club's supervisor of trails in 1926, Karl Pomeroy Harrington, similarly remarked upon "the ever-lengthening procession of tchug-tchugging automobiles [which] rushes madly up through the Crawford Notch and down through the Franconia Notch—or perchance takes them in reverse order—and through the clouds of dust and the effluvia of gasoline the languid passengers are dimly conscious of a blurred moving picture of wooded ridges and dashing streams."[324] What tourists wanted, but Harrington did not say, was a leisurely tramp through the Flume.

MARKETING THE FLUME

In contrast to the Flume House, which was heavily advertised during the late nineteenth century, the Flume was not. What advertising existed was aimed at filling the hotel and not driving visitation to the gorge. Consequently, hotel advertisements, which generally consisted of small classified items inserted in regional papers, made little or no mention of the Flume.[325] By the last decade of the century, however, increasing reference to and images of the chasm were employed to promote both the Flume House and Profile House. "When you drive to the Flume, do not take lunch, but go to the Flume House and get one of the best dinners in the mountains for $1," exhorted advertisements from 1899. "The Flume House is also one of the most attractive houses in the mountains for a long stay," they added.[326]

The rise in automobile tourism, however, was accompanied by an increase in tourist literature specifically related to the Flume, directed toward motorists who were unlikely to make an extended stay but wished to see the region's attractions. The Profile and Flume Hotels Company produced marketing, as did the State of New Hampshire, all including notice of the Flume, in an effort to tap into its tourist dollar potential. By the 1920s, images of the Flume regularly appeared in advertising for the upscale Profile House.

Not only did prospective visitors desire to see images of the Flume, but those who did view it wished to have souvenir images of their own. Picture postcards became popular following 1898, and hundreds bearing different views of the Flume flooded the market and found a ready sale. During August 1920, over fifty-six thousand postcards of the Old Man of the Mountain were sold at the Profile Lake gift shop, and numbers for the Flume were likely not far behind, an indication of the volume done in these items.[327] Not only did postcards represent an inexpensive keepsake, but those that traveled through the postal system brought awareness of the Flume to all who handled them. Postcard publishers often compiled these same images into larger souvenir booklets for sale, the Flume nearly always figuring in at least one view.

Many visitors preferred capturing their own more personal images. With the introduction of the inexpensive Kodak Brownie box camera in 1900, photography became so popular that Flume House manager Seth R. Elliott felt compelled to provide amateur photographers with a dark room. Many of their images captured individuals standing in the Flume with the chasm as a mere backdrop. Journalist and photographer A.H. Beardsley was uncertain why amateur photographers ignored the scenery

THE FLUME, WHITE MTS., N. H.

Right: Woman with Avalanche Falls as a backdrop, photograph, 1915. *Author's collection.*

Below: J.V. Hartman & Co. *In the Flume, Franconia Notch, White Mountains, N.H.*, lithographic postcard, circa 1920. *Author's collection.*

Opposite: E.D. Putnam & Sons. *The Flume, White Mts., N.H.*, real photo postcard, circa 1910. *Author's collection.*

around them. "Why it is that thousands of vacationists who come to New Hampshire bring cameras and appear to confine their picture-making to members of their own party or to John in the boat or Mabel frying a doughnut, I am unable to say....I do deplore limiting picture-making to those subjects which in a short time, usually lose their interest. But a good photograph of Franconia Notch, The Flume, or of Echo Lake may be a joy forever."[328] What Beardsley missed was precisely the same criticism that intellectuals of an earlier generation had levied, that the Flume had become for many a social rather than an introspective space. In 1926, one Flume visitor reported, "Never saw so many cameras in operation at one time. Everybody, it seemed, was taking pictures of his or her particular party, with the towering walls of the Flume as a background."[329]

FLUME TEA HOUSE

On June 27, 1918, the Flume House, the locus of activity for the Flume since its construction, was destroyed by fire. Having opened for the season just two weeks earlier, it became the third hotel at the site to be burned. Flames were discovered on the roof, and without fire apparatus or equipment other than buckets, little could be done to save the building. The hotel's thirty guests escaped and there was sufficient time to salvage their personal belongings, as well as "most of the hotel furniture."[330] Insurance covered only a portion of the estimated $75,000 loss.

Ironically, destruction of the Flume House, which had been so closely wedded to the development of the Flume as a tourist attraction, helped solidify the purely recreational aspect of the chasm. While people had once traveled to the Flume House for accommodation and meals and used it as a base for explorations farther afield, visits to the area going forward would be strictly recreational and revolve nearly exclusively around the Flume.

Nonetheless, day-trippers still expected services, and to accommodate them Colonel Charles H. Greenleaf constructed the Flume Tea House in mid-1919 directly across the notch road from the former hotel site and immediately adjacent to the Flume Path. The building, which used salvaged brick from the Flume House's chimneys, was designed and its construction superintended by Greenleaf. Its appearance was deceptive. Although it resembled a single-story building from the outside, the teahouse included two stories with a lunch counter, restaurant, private

Detroit Publishing Company. *The Flume T House, White Mts., N.H.*, lithographic postcard, circa 1920. *Author's collection.*

dining room, souvenir shop and restrooms on the first floor; and six guest rooms, four staff bedrooms, a bathroom and linen and broom closets on the second floor. The "six attractive double sleeping rooms [were] for the accommodation of belated tourists" and were claimed by the *White Mountain Echo* to be as well appointed as rooms at the luxurious Profile House.[331]

On August 29, 1919, the Flume Tea House opened with a housewarming and tea attended by members of the Profile House hotel and cottage "colony," with musical selections by the Profile Symphony Orchestra. The *New York Sun* described the opening, which drew some three hundred automobilists, as "the event of the season" alongside reopening of the Forest Hills Hotel at Franconia, which had been closed for two years.[332] A year after the teahouse's opening, the *White Mountain Echo* reported a week in August 1920 when over one thousand visited.[333]

The construction of the Flume Tea House (later known in a concession to modernity as the Flume T House) was significant in the recreational development of the Flume as it reflected a shift in what amenities tourists expected and marked a transitional phase between the Flume House and the present visitors' center. No longer were long-term accommodations provided. Instead, the teahouse was intended for motorists who might like to tour the Flume, enjoy a quick and inexpensive meal and purchase souvenirs through which to remember their outing. Despite its name, tea was not a focus; the teahouse instead reflected a social movement of the time that sought to cater to traveling Americans' desire for wholesome and inexpensive meals in clean establishments.

CHAPTER 7

"WAYS AND MEANS OF EXTRACTING THE FAST NICKEL"

THE ABBOTT YEARS, 1921–1928

COMMERCIALIZING THE FLUME

In April 1921, a radical change occurred for the Flume when the property of the Profile and Flume Hotels Company—which included not only the Flume and Flume Tea House but also the Pool, the Basin, the Old Man of the Mountain, the Profile House and over six thousand acres of forested land stretching nine miles through Franconia Notch—was acquired by the Frank H. Abbott and Son Hotel Company. Following the sale, Abbott and his son Karl P. Abbott named their new holdings Greenleaf Park in recognition of their former owner, Charles H. Greenleaf, who was a firm proponent of forest reservations and had done so much to preserve Franconia Notch in a relatively pristine state.

Karl P. Abbott, a hotelier his entire life, recognized the commercial value of the Flume as a tourist attraction. In August 1920, the *White Mountain Echo* reported that the Flume was attracting as many as one thousand people a day. Abbott, looking to tap into the boom in outdoor recreation that followed World War I, believed that the profits from the enterprise had not yet been fully realized, and he set out to do so.[334]

Abbott's regard for the Flume as a largely commercial venture is reflected in the language used in his 1950 memoir, *Open for the Season.* "It was all interesting…," Abbott wrote, "figuring out ways and means of extracting the fast nickel from the pockets of the traveling public." He mentions concessions manager Frank C. Brace, who "was always thinking up gimmicks and gadgets to sell to the tourists," including five-cent cellophane-wrapped maple sugar cakes. "I saw a chance to increase the company's profits and built a large gate at the entrance of the tollgate, put in automatic turnstiles, and hired pretty girls as gatetenders."[335] Abbott also added and heavily promoted gift shops, one of which was located at the Flume, and named them the Profile Wonder Shops. Photographer Charles Allen was engaged in 1926 for $5,000 to take images of the region that were used for promotional purposes, and for the 1928 and 1929 seasons, Allen secured the concession to take photographs of Flume visitors with the background of their choice.[336]

Abbott remained dismissive of the Profile and Flume Hotels Company's efforts prior to 1921, when the company had "questioned [its] right to maintain the toll road [into the Flume] and had made very little to-do about it. They had a man at the entrance with a little green bag who charged five cents to go into the Flume."[337] What Abbott perceived as legal uncertainty and colorless promotion was more likely hesitancy on the part of Greenleaf to over-commercialize the Flume.

C.T. Bodwell. *Entrance to Flume Gate, Flume, N.H.*, real photo postcard, 1933. *Author's collection.*

Abbott writes that Flume revenue jumped during the first season under his ownership from no more than $3,000 to $30,000 and ultimately within three years to $100,000 for all notch concessions combined.[338] Profitability at the Flume was driven by increasing visitation. Tourists were undeterred by the admission hike to twenty-five cents, with 75,000 visiting in 1923 and more than 100,000 in 1924.[339] One newspaper in 1926 reported the Flume as attracting more visitors than ever before, and such visits were made more practical by the mid-1920s boom in overnight auto camps along the Daniel Webster Highway between Plymouth and Franconia Notch.[340] "There's a wooden shack beside the highway waiting for them. It is about 10 feet long by 8 feet wide, and it contains a comfortable bed and a chair or two and an electric lamp. Barely room enough to turn around in. But there's generally a table and a settee outside, and there's a good view, and a food shop at hand, and running water. And it's most inviting at the close of a long day of touring."[341] Day-trippers, excursionists from the region's remaining resort hotels and outings from the White Mountains' children's camps all visited the Flume, prompting Abbott to expand the souvenir shop and rebuild the Flume road.[342]

Commodification of the Flume, however, upset many who even prior to this date had argued that the chasm was being degraded by excessive visitation fueled by unfettered commercialization. A purportedly humorous piece in the *White Mountain Echo* in August 1903 nonetheless had a serious point to make suggesting that the heavily trafficked Flume paled in comparison to the more rugged though smaller Kinsman Flume and faulting the Franconia Notch gorge for the presence of the wooden walkways (pejoratively referred to as "scaffolding"), lack of mosses and surfeit of tourists.[343] Such a heretical view of the Flume was not yet widely held, and the *Echo* insisted that the Flume "never loses its popularity as 'one of the chief sights of the mountains.'"[344] Nonetheless, commercialization was taking a toll.

Though few explicitly said so, Abbott's efforts to squeeze as much profit as possible from the Flume appeared comparable to earlier efforts by timber companies to monetize and extract the maximum value from Franconia Notch. An August 1922 article in the Plymouth, New Hampshire *Record* headlined "A New Way of Profiteering" railed against Abbott's commercialization of the Flume.[345] Hobart Pillsbury, writing for the *Republican Champion* in Newport, New Hampshire, warned readers that "many of the most beautiful spots in the White mountains have already been profaned by commercial invasion....The Flume has recently been made a 'concession.' Souvenir and refreshment stands are all too common for the admirers of

Detroit Publishing Company. *Franconia Notch, in the Flume, White Mts., N.H.*, glass negative, circa 1895. *Courtesy of the Library of Congress.*

primeval mountain beauty."[346] Another correspondent to the *Littleton Courier*, E.E. Woodbury of Woodstock, reflected the criticisms of many when he argued against the commodification of the Flume and the notch's other attractions. We "object to taking such God given beauties as those furnished us in the Franconia Notch for profiteering purposes," he wrote in 1924.[347]

Woodbury's solution was that the state needed to acquire title to Franconia Notch in order to protect it not only from lumbering but also from the threat of commercialization. "There seems to be no rules or regulations as to management of camp sites or parking places. The beautiful forests are left to the mercy of careless campers and many of them have no mercy. The only semblance of any particular care or interest on the part of the owners is at the Flume."[348] In rebuttal, Abbott argued that boosting revenue was necessary for the upkeep of the Flume and Greenleaf Park, noting that the hotel company provided access, including camping and hiking facilities, at no cost to the public.[349]

SAVING THE FLUME

The question of state ownership of the Flume was ultimately forced by the destruction of the Profile House by a fire of undetermined origin on August 3, 1923. Rather than rebuild their hotel, the Abbotts chose to place the entirety of the Profile and Flume Hotels Company's holdings on the market, and for the second time in as many years, the Flume and all of surrounding Franconia Notch was up for sale. A five-year effort to save the notch and its attractions followed, with the State of New Hampshire and Society for the Protection of New Hampshire Forests jointly acquiring title in 1928.

The story of saving Franconia Notch has been too well told elsewhere to be repeated here.[350] Karl Abbott oversimplifies the effort, writing that he merely acceded to his father's view that Franconia Notch should be a state park and accordingly sold it to the state.[351] New Hampshire, however, did not secure its purchase option until 1925, during which time the Abbotts considered various alternatives to recoup their losses, including the sale of timber rights in the notch. At the time, the estimated value of the notch, including standing timber and tourist concessions (derived principally from the Flume operation), was estimated at $500,000 by the Abbotts and the *Manchester Union*, though Governor John Winant placed the figure as low as $225,000.[352] Ultimately, the state agreed to purchase the notch for a forest reservation and state park under the management of the forestry commission in order to protect Franconia Notch's woodlands and scenery. A purchase price of $400,000 was agreed upon, half provided by state allocation and the remainder to be raised through public subscription.[353]

Partnering with the state was the Society for the Protection of New Hampshire Forests (Forest Society), founded in 1901with the purpose of "seeking to perpetuate the forests of New Hampshire through their wise use

Paul R. Jenks. *Harold D. Miller (Trails Foreman); William L. Starr, Jr.; Fred Fish; Bachus; Harland P. Sisk; William J. Henrich; and* [unknown] *with their trail crew tools in the Flume, Franconia Notch, N.H., on a Summer Day*, glass lantern slide, 1924. *Courtesy of the Appalachian Mountain Club Library & Archives.*

and their complete reservation in places of special scenic beauty."[354] The society entered into direct negotiations with the Profile and Flume Hotels Company in 1924 with the aim of preventing commercial timber cutting in Franconia Notch and protecting its scenic beauty. Spurred on by Philip W. Ayres (1861–1945), the society's first forester, and supported by various state and region-wide organizations such as the New Hampshire Federation of Women's Clubs, New Hampshire Grange and the Appalachian Mountain Club, the society spearheaded the $200,000 fundraising campaign. Ayres insisted upon a direct purchase rather than a mortgage on the property, arguing that the latter would promote further commercialization of the Flume as a means to repay the loan.

Ayres, who had been influential in the establishment of the White Mountain National Forest, was persuasive in encouraging thousands to contribute to the preservation of Franconia Notch, including the Flume and Pool. Tom Bodwell, director of the Flume Reservation from 1928 to 1947, later acknowledged the debt owed Ayres for his role in saving Franconia Notch. In a handwritten letter, Bodwell told Ayres, "New Hampshire and all of us owe you more than mere dollars can settle for."[355]

Though the Old Man of the Mountain featured prominently in the fundraising campaign and this association helped solidify its identity with the state at the expense of the Flume (which previously had been the attraction most identifiable with Franconia Notch), the Flume nonetheless held a central

Governor Huntley Spaulding of New Hampshire (left) *with ex-Governor Percival Baxter of Maine,* photograph, 1928. Both were instrumental in the establishment of iconic parks in their respective states. *Author's collection.*

place in negotiations, for it was the attraction generating the most return and its revenue-bearing capacity was viewed as a considerable financial asset.[356] The *Milford Cabinet* in an editorial in early 1928 in fact argued that the state's effort to acquire Franconia Notch was not for preservation purposes, as the timber was never seriously threatened, but was aimed at securing the Flume as a financial asset. "It is a relief," remarked the newspaper, "that those in charge of the plans have finally admitted that what they need $400,000 to buy is not 6,000 acres of rough land, not timber, but two souvenir stores and a toll-road and gate leading to the Flume."[357] While the opinion was pure cynicism on the part of the paper, there was reluctance by its owners to part with the Flume financially. As part of the final agreement, the Abbotts retained the concessions at the Flume for two years—1928 and 1929—in order to compensate them for the $100,000 more they had sought but did not receive as their asking price for Franconia Notch.

Meanwhile, an agreement signed between the state and the Forest Society on June 6, 1928, authorized the society to hold title to 913 acres at the southern end of the notch, including the Flume and the Pool. Designated shortly thereafter as the Flume Reservation, this property was to be conveyed to the state on or before December 31, 1947.[358] During the interim, the society was permitted to operate the attractions following the 1929 season and use the revenue for furthering forestry interests in the state and restoring the Flume Reservation to what Ayres referred to as "its primeval beauty."[359] This arrangement was made in part as the state felt it then lacked the expertise necessary to administer a recreational operation catering to up to 100,000 visitors annually, whereas the society had operated the Lost River Reservation at nearby Kinsman Notch since 1912.[360] Governor Huntley N. Spaulding was also hesitant about placing control of the Flume Reservation under the political jurisdiction of Concord legislators.

CHAPTER 8

"THE MOST IMPORTANT PART OF THE WORK IS TO SERVE THE PUBLIC"

THE FOREST SOCIETY YEARS, 1928–1947

THE FLUME RESERVATION

Having helped secure Franconia Notch's future, the Forest Society nearly immediately began implementation of its forest preservation plan for the Flume Reservation while continuing to promote low-impact usage there. To head the reservation, the society selected as its director Clare Thomas "Tom" Bodwell (1893–1976), who had been associated with the society's earlier reservation at Lost River and was engaged as estate manager for Colonel Isaac N. Lewis's Fernbrook Farm at Bethlehem. Bodwell would guide the Flume Reservation for the following twenty years. Deeply committed to his role, Bodwell had a clear vision of the Forest Society's mission at the Flume, telling society president Lawrence Rathbun in 1935 that he considered "the most important part of the work is to serve the public in such a way as to make friends, not only for Franconia Notch and the White Mountains, but for New Hampshire and New England as a whole."[361]

Though the Profile and Flume Hotels Company managed the attractions during the 1928 and 1929 seasons and employed twenty-five people at the Flume to do so, Forest Society personnel were also on the reservation grounds to assist visitors. Though Bodwell acknowledges that Karl Abbott was accommodating, there appears to have been some friction between the hotel company and the Forest Society that owned the property over the manner in which the Flume concession was operated. Bodwell was critical of the hotel company's lax grounds maintenance, noting the need in his daily record book for 1928 for it to properly dispose of garbage and rubbish.[362] Additionally, Bodwell felt that the hotel company was not forthcoming with information. "Would like to know how many people paid admission to Flume to-day [July 6, 1928]. Everyone here is very close mouthed and knows nothing about numbers entering, etc."[363] Bodwell also disagreed with the hotel company's policy of charging a separate admission to the Pool, noting that it discouraged visitation. From these observations, Bodwell formulated a series of improvements to protect the reservation and enhance the visitor experience to be implemented once the society assumed full control in 1930.

VISITOR VOLUME

Under the management of the Profile and Flume Hotels Company and the later direction of the Forest Society, the Flume remained popular and profitable. During one hour on the Sunday before Labor Day 1928, 800 people were admitted, and Bodwell estimated the day's attendance at 6,000.[364] By 1933, in the midst of the Depression, an estimated 100,000 were visiting annually.[365] Labor Day 1935 was so popular that 200 motorists were unable to find parking, and the total number of visits for that year was 98,429, an increase of 16,594 over 1934.[366]

Concessions contributed to the Flume's revenue. "The soda fountain does a tremendous business as does the tea room and gift shop," Bodwell noted in 1928. "The store up in the Flume also is a money maker."[367] Bodwell also noted higher volumes on hot days, while the number of lunches and dinners served every day prompted him to marvel, "The cook is a wonder." Throughout the 1930s, the Flume Tea House continued to provide simple fare consisting of soups, sandwiches, desserts and other light refreshment. Social historian Jan Whitaker in her exploration of the early twentieth-century teahouse movement noted that "tea room cooks apparently felt any recipe could be improved with the addition of liberal amounts of butter, cream, and mayonnaise. The sandwich, the salad, and the casserole came to their own on tea room menus, and home-style desserts were perfected and made elegant."[368] Surviving Flume Tea House menus from the period indicate that this was indeed the type of fare offered Flume visitors.

To direct large flows of traffic on peak days in the early 1930s, the reservation operated a "Flume Traffic Squad" composed of Boy Scouts from throughout

The Flume on a Busy Day, showing the Flume Tea House and entrance gate, photograph, 1929. *Author's collection.*

the state. Nine scouts were put to work on Labor Day 1930, one of whom, Eagle Scout William J. Thompson Jr., reported: "The parking areas, holding 500 cars, filled up early in the morning and stayed filled until nightfall. The traffic poured through in a steady stream all day. The Scouts had a difficult piece of work to do in parking cars, letting cars into line, and keeping the hill clear so that cars would not bump each other....We did not have one jam all day."[369] Travelers (as noted by their license plates) came from all states, while a register kept for years at the Boulder Cabin recorded guests from faraway lands. For those coming by auto, gasoline was available at the Flume.

Throughout the Depression, the Flume operation continued to warrant its characterization as a moneymaker. Cash receipts of $95,570.19 (1932) and $86,130.30 (1933) for Flume admissions and the concessions managed by the Forest Society reflect this.[370] Often overlooked, however, was the value of the Flume to the local economy. During three successive years in the early 1930s, the Flume Reservation returned collectively just over $117,000 in wages and payment for supplies and materials to Lincoln, North Woodstock, Franconia and other communities.[371] In 1934, three-quarters of the Flume staff were from New Hampshire, and surviving correspondence from 1933 documents efforts made by the Forest Society to employ local residents, an important consideration given that the nation was then in the depths of the Depression.[372]

NEW PATHS

Upon the society's acquisition of the Flume in 1928, Bodwell began planning improvements to provide better access, improve safety and enhance enjoyment of the reservation, though work on these projects was deferred until 1930, when the Forest Society assumed charge of the reservation and secured the Flume receipts with which to finance them. Most conspicuous of these improvements was the creation of a new trail system. Bodwell proposed construction of a unified network that would open new areas and establish a single route through the reservation, enabling guests to exit without the need to backtrack. Roughly composed of three trails, Bodwell referred to this network informally as the Triangle Trail from its three-sided course as depicted on a map.[373]

Construction on these new trails commenced in the early 1930s and was completed for the 1935 season. Trail-building was performed manually and proved arduous. "Gravel for the footpaths is being bucked up the steep trail on the backs of workmen, and the job is slow, tedious and costly," remarked the *Manchester Union* in September 1934, "but will insure new mountain pleasures and well known Flume safety."[374]

Previously, guests arriving at the Flume had hiked the gravel road through the woods and over the Flume Covered Bridge to the chasm. Those not wishing to do so could, for a quarter, travel by bus as far as Boulder Cabin, from which it was a short uphill walk. In order to provide a safer route for pedestrians and one that allowed them to avoid the dust kicked up by the buses, a new path from the Flume gate to the end of the bus road named the Boulder Cabin Path was cut. The path partially paralleled the bus road and crossed the Flume Covered Bridge. It incorporated portions of the earlier carriage road and passed near a great glacial erratic named the Great Boulder.

The Rim Path (1933) running from the top of Table Rock along the northern rim of the gorge to the head of the Flume afforded views from above. Bodwell's purpose in cutting this trail was to relieve congestion in the Flume below on high visitation days and to provide a direct return path to the teahouse from the top of the Flume for visitors wishing to view the gorge only, Bodwell acknowledging that "people do not like to walk any further than necessary to see the main features."[375] He suggested the name Sunset Rim Trail as the path ran westward toward the setting sun.

Linking the Rim Path with the Pool was a 0.7-mile path shown on a 1933 plan as the Rimpool Path, referred to in Bodwell's notes as the

Above: C.T. Bodwell. *The Boulder Cabin Trail, Flume, N.H.*, real photo postcard, 1933. The trail is depicted shortly after its completion. *Author's collection.*

Right: Flume Reservation. *Rim Trail, Flume Gorge, N.H.*, real photo postcard, 1933. *Author's collection.*

Flume-Pool Path and today known as the Ridge Path. This path appears not to have been completed until the mid-1930s and replaced the path that had formerly run along the east bank of the Pemigewasset from the covered bridge to the Pool that may have been the path originally cut by John Merrill. Bodwell's Ridge Path ran through delightful pine woods before descending by means of a log stairway to the Pemigewasset, which was crossed by a small bridge.

The third path running between the Pool and the entrance gate, the Wildwood Path, was also a half mile long and led "through glacier bowlders and forest growth to the highway near the entrance to the Flume."[376] The boulders had been deposited twenty-five thousand years earlier when the last great ice sheet receded. The path followed the likely course of the original trail to the Pool that had been cut nearly a century earlier.

Construction of these paths permitted for the first time a circuitous route linking the Flume and the Pool and resulted in the first maps of the Flume being printed; these continue to be distributed to each guest. Those distributed in the 1950s and later had delightful line drawings of the features at each location. Bodwell determined that in the first year, 20 percent of visitors used the new trail system.[377] Among these was First Lady Eleanor Roosevelt, who made an informal visit on the morning of August 16, 1935, walking the entire two and a half miles of the "new Flume trail, just completed."[378]

The wooden walkway through the Flume was also reconstructed at this time. Built in three-hundred-foot sections that could be removed at the end of the season, the walkway was reinstalled each spring, which helped extend its life. "The ancient board walk in the Flume has been removed," announced the *Boston Globe* in 1933, "and in its place for some distance is a path [Gorge Path] close to the brook running through the gorge, to a point where the walls rise. From there on a new board walk, less conspicuous than the old, follows the contours of the gorge."[379]

To accommodate tourists visiting during inclement weather, rain shelters were constructed sometime after the mid-1930s at the base and head of the Flume, at Liberty Gorge and above the Pool.[380] The sign at the gate was redone to include two images of the Flume in order to alleviate the persistent question, "What is the Flume?" that Bodwell found was asked by nine out of every ten people, an indication that the gorge was less well known nationally than it once had been. Bodwell intended for the revamped sign to provide passersby with the answer and entice them to visit.[381] And they did. During the mid-1930s, with many American families

C.T. Bodwell. *Log Stairway on Rimpool Path, Flume, N.H.*, real photo postcard, 1936. *Author's collection.*

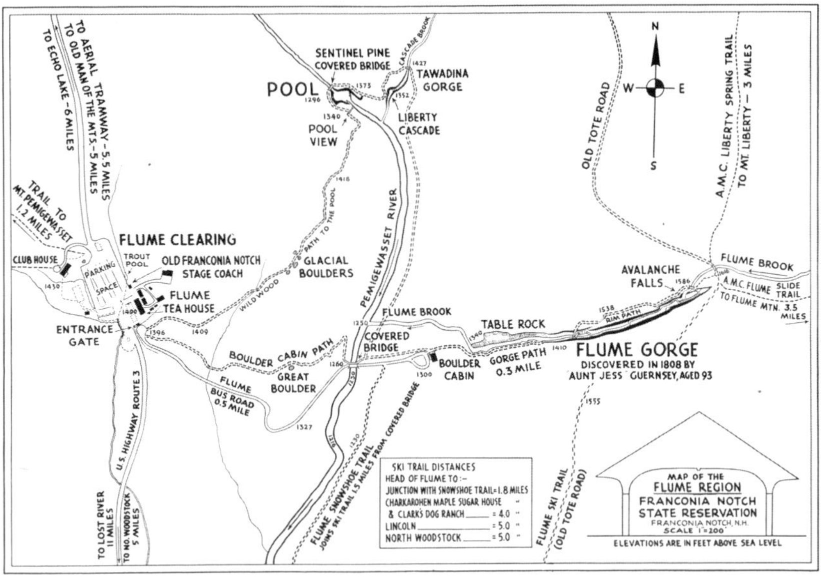

Above: Flume Reservation. *Map of the Flume*, circa 1934. *Author's collection.*

Left: Flume Reservation. *New Flume Gorge Path, Franconia Notch, White Mts., N.H.*, lithographic postcard, circa 1935. *Author's collection.*

struggling financially, the Flume afforded an easy and inexpensive day's recreation. Visitation in August 1936 was reported as up 26 percent over the previous year, and 1937 showed a not insubstantial 16 percent increase on top of that.[382]

"NEW DISCOVERIES"

Bodwell's trail system was also laid out to take advantage of new scenic attractions within the reservation. One of these was Liberty Gorge, which Bodwell recorded in his day book for 1928:

> *New Discovery….Several hundred feet down the Pemigewasset River from the Pool and on the south-eastern side of the gorge is a deep cut in the ridge. Following up the brook (too small to attract fishermen) I discovered a beautiful and impressive gorge with a series of fine and lovely water falls of great height in all. I say discover purposely—for while no doubt this gorge was seen by the lumbermen many years ago—I have been unable to find a single person connected with the Hotel Company or with the Notch, who has ever seen or heard of the place. Though smaller and less impressive than the Flume, it is nevertheless a feature of great attraction.*[383]

In fact, the cascade had been known at least by 1898, when Frank O. Carpenter mentioned it in his *Guide Book to the Franconia Notch and Pemigewasset Valley.* Known then as Langton Cascades, the feature appears to have gone unvisited and was forgotten, likely as there was no path that accessed it.[384]

So that visitors could view the cascade, Bodwell located the Ridge Trail across the upper end of the gorge, for which he sought "a suitable Indian name," eventually settling on Tawadina Gorge, Abenaki for "mountain gorge and stream."[385] Though it appears on one early Flume trail map under this name, Tawadina Gorge was shortly afterward renamed Liberty Gorge.

Another feature of the reservation popularized by Bodwell was a singular pine tree standing nearly 175 feet high, 16 feet in circumference at the base and 5 feet in diameter and situated on a cliff above the Pool. Bodwell named it the Sentinel Pine, "for there in silence and solitude it seems to stand guard over all."[386] The tree, whose top reached 305 feet above the Pemigewasset River, was a remarkable site and a reminder of New Hampshire's colonial past, when such pines had been reserved for use as masts by the Royal Navy.

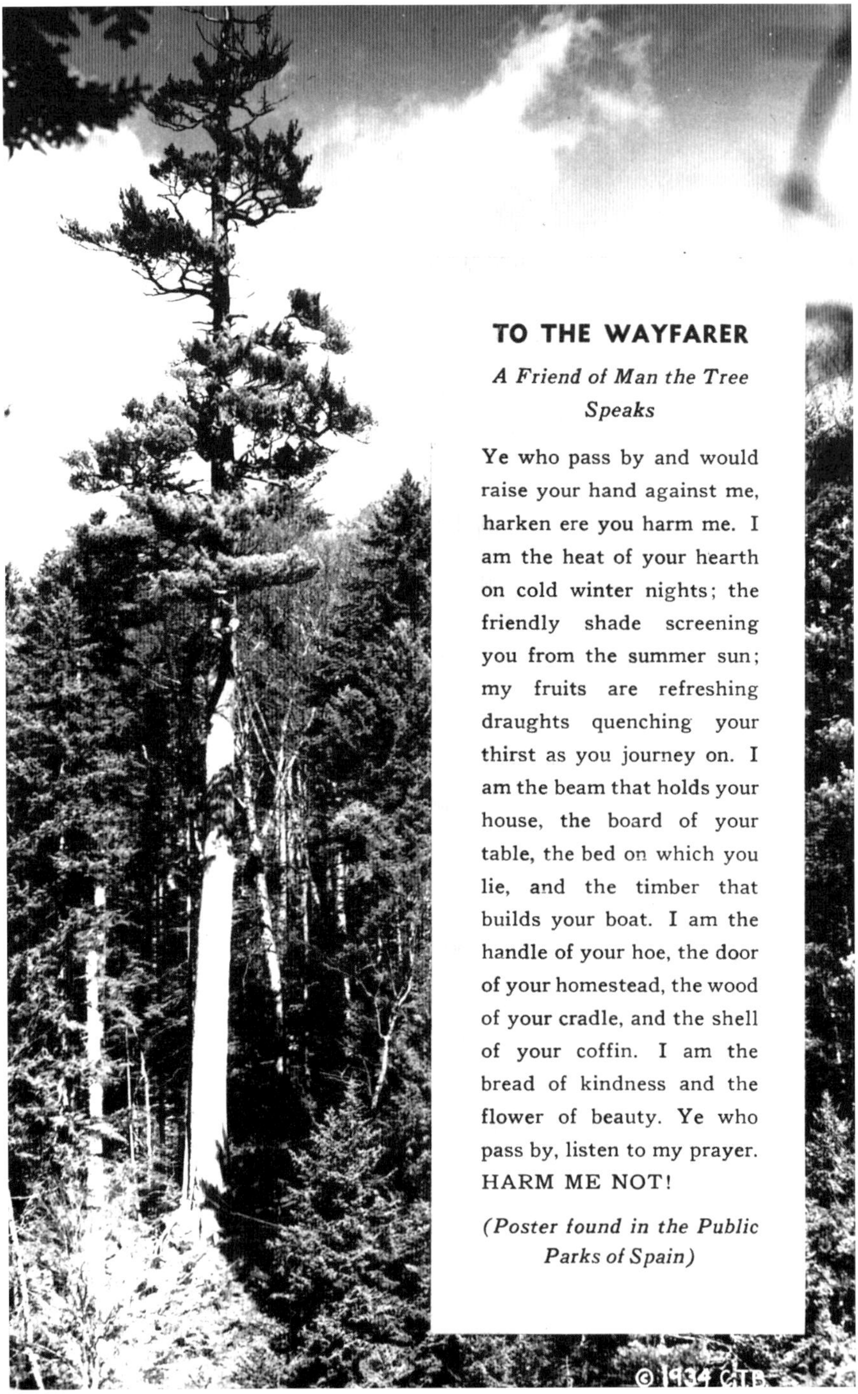
TO THE WAYFARER
A Friend of Man the Tree Speaks
Ye who pass by and would raise your hand against me, harken ere you harm me. I am the heat of your hearth on cold winter nights; the friendly shade screening you from the summer sun; my fruits are refreshing draughts quenching your thirst as you journey on. I am the beam that holds your house, the board of your table, the bed on which you lie, and the timber that builds your boat. I am the handle of your hoe, the door of your homestead, the wood of your cradle, and the shell of your coffin. I am the bread of kindness and the flower of beauty. Ye who pass by, listen to my prayer. HARM ME NOT!
(Poster found in the Public Parks of Spain)
© 1934 CTB

Right: C.T. Bodwell. *Liberty Cascades in Liberty Gorge, Flume, N.H.*, lithographic postcard, 1936. *Author's collection.*

Opposite: Flume Reservation. *Sentinel Pine on Flume-Pool Path, Franconia Notch, White Mts., N.H.*, real photo postcard, 1934. *Author's collection.*

The tree, later determined to be three hundred years old, was the subject of various news features and photos, which Bodwell hoped would draw attention to the Flume Reservation.[387] Significantly, a photograph of the tree and not the Flume appears on the 1933 map of the reservation.

NEW BUILDINGS

Other improvements undertaken during Bodwell's directorship targeted the site's existing buildings.

The terminus of the roadway into the Flume had since the late 1800s been the location of a rest station that also sold souvenirs and refreshments. In 1921, according to a North Woodstock trail guide, it housed the Flume Café "at the end of the road" where souvenirs could be purchased. By 1934, the building was in such disrepair that Bodwell called for its replacement.

Work commenced on a new structure known as Boulder Cabin the following year, and it opened on June 13, 1936.[388] In addition to serving its former purpose selling souvenirs, the cabin also housed the wooden bridge model now located in the visitors' center.

Though relatively new, the Flume Tea House at the Flume entrance was considered inadequate for the ever-increasing visitor volume, and Bodwell informed Forest Society president Allen Hollis in 1936 that a new building was sorely needed. "Much additional business that we now lose could be secured, in addition to old friends who would come back and visit us to see the new building."[389] Instead of replacing the structure, construction on a new auxiliary building, the Flume Clubhouse, located on the west side of the highway near the former Flume House site, was begun in 1937 and completed the following year. Built as an administration building housing a clubhouse, dormitory and offices, the building was designed by the firm of Arthur A. Shurcliff and Sidney N. Shurcliff of Boston and constructed at a cost of $50,000.

The clubhouse was intended to demonstrate that lower grades of native lumber, when combined with good craftsmanship and employing wood,

C.T. Bodwell. *Old Franconia Notch Stage Coach, White Mts., N.H.*, real photo postcard, 1933. The coach is Abbot-Downing number 431. *Author's collection.*

granite and fieldstone sourced from throughout New Hampshire, could produce an appealing and economical structure. The building was framed with red spruce, and its recreation room featured adze-hewn white pine beams. Its fourteen rooms were paneled in sound-knotted white pine and had floors of red oak milled at Concord. To cover the roof, two men took nine weeks to split, trim and shave some forty thousand white pine shingles produced from old-growth pines harvested at Franconia and Landaff. The shingles were twenty-eight inches in length and one inch thick at the butt. Yellow birch furniture made at Milford furnished the clubhouse, while the grounds were landscaped with locally indigenous plants.

Other support buildings were constructed at this time as well, including a small wood canopy structure to house the Abbot-Downing stagecoach that had been built in 1874 and was purchased by the Forest Society in 1934. A relic of the previous century, the Concord-built stagecoach had carried passengers from Plymouth to locations in Franconia Notch, including the Flume and Profile Houses, until 1911 and provided a stark contrast to the automobiles that now easily brought visitors to the Flume for the day.[390] For years left in its original condition, the stage was later restored at the behest of the Lincoln Bicentennial Committee and former New Hampshire first lady Mrs. Sherman Adams in the 1960s. The stage now occupies a prominent place within the Flume visitors' center.

PROMOTION

While the Forest Society inherited a commercialized Flume operation, it made efforts to upgrade the operation and eliminate those aspects that might cheapen it, ensuring that promotion of the gorge was both tasteful and educational. Much of Bodwell's winter each year was taken up with securing goods to sell at the Flume Reservation and the other gift shops within Franconia Notch State Park for which the Forest Society also held the concession. "People are interested in fine merchandise at a reasonable price," Bodwell informed Philip Ayres.[391] Postcards were the most popular keepsake, easy to carry home and inexpensive. In 1933, 108,146 postcards were sold in the reservation's gift shops at the cost of two for a nickel.[392]

Many of the images appearing on the reservation's attractive black-and-white postcards were taken by Bodwell himself, and they reveal him to have been a skilled photographer. Successful sales of these cards encouraged

Left: C.T. Bodwell. *The Flume*, real photo postcard, circa 1934. *Author's collection.*

Below: C.T. Bodwell. *'Sipsis' (Bird) Flume Abenaki Indian Basket Maker*, real photo postcard, 1934. The Flume Tea House is in the background. *Author's collection.*

Bodwell to purchase a secondhand Zeiss Ikon 5x7 view camera for $215 in 1934.[393] "All photographic works would be of a much finer quality when made from new pictures taken with this much larger and finer camera," he assured Ayres.[394]

The type and number of souvenirs carried was broad. While decorative china and porcelain were still staples, beautiful hand-tinted prints by Charles H. Sawyer and high-quality Native American baskets, many secured from the Abenaki and Penobscot tribes, were also sold. In 1939, a portion of the gift shop was set aside for the League of New Hampshire Craftsmen, an organization founded in 1932 to support handcrafts in the state.

Consistent with its goal to promote the interests of forestry within New Hampshire, the Forest Society used the Flume Reservation to support its educational initiatives. Regular forestry conferences were held at the Flume Clubhouse, and in 1933, the reservation was put to use as an outdoor laboratory for summer campers at the New Hampshire Nature Camp held at Lost River under the auspices of the society. The Flume Reservation also operated a nursery in the 1930s, likely propagating plants for use throughout Franconia Notch.

THE FLUME IN WINTER

The Forest Society during the 1930s was also instrumental in developing the Flume as a winter sports center, albeit short-lived. During its first hundred years, the Flume had remained a seasonal attraction, largely because the notch road remained impassable in winter but also since skiing and snowshoeing had not yet gained popularity. The severity of the weather in Franconia Notch was also a factor, with nineteenth-century reports recording extreme cold—as in 1836, when the temperature was reported to have plunged to fifty below zero, and the following year when it dropped to thirty-five below—as well as deep snow in many years.[395] Finally, hotels were not equipped to cater to winter tourists, which at times caused dissatisfaction. In March 1884, the refusal of the Flume House to accommodate a late-winter party of tourists from Boston reached newspapers as far away as Wisconsin.[396]

Yet though difficult to access in winter, the Flume was recognized for the beauty of its ice-covered walls at that time of year. Starr King suggested that the winter scenery at the Flume was "more startling" than that of summer and stated that stereoscopic views taken in winter would confirm

Top: Bierstadt Brothers. *Winter View in the Flume, Franconia Mts., N.H.*, albumen silver print stereograph, circa 1860. *Courtesy of the Miriam and Ira D. Wallach Division of Art, Print and Photographs: Photography Collection, New York Public Library.*

Bottom: S.F. Adams. *View in the Flume (Winter)*, albumen silver print stereograph, circa 1875. *Courtesy of the Miriam and Ira D. Wallach Division of Art, Print and Photographs: Photography Collection, New York Public Library.*

his assertion.[397] In his 1859 guidebook, Samuel C. Eastman opined that "in all seasons, it is a place for study, for reflection and delight."[398]

While intrepid adventurers did seek out the Flume under its cover of snow, including members of the Appalachian Mountain and Dartmouth Outing Clubs who made winter excursions to the region in the late nineteenth century, it was only in the early 1900s that others began to participate as more and more gained proficiency on skis and snowshoes. One of these was Paul R. Jenks, who spent a winter at the turn of the last century in Franconia Notch, making sure to visit the Flume, which for him proved unforgettable, where "one could catch the secret of a winter nightfall."

> *The winter Flume is not for the transient visitor, to be explored in a few minutes and abandoned as "done." Walks and railings are useless, for the snow slopes down over them, and every foothold must be broken out level. The snow is not as deep as in the woods, perhaps three feet. You can climb up through the cleft, but I would rather not. Of all Nature's winter shrines there is none I desire to hold in mind undisturbed by the snowshoe print so much as this. Let us stand at the entrance and look and feel, and quietly turn away. For there is a sense of solitude not felt in summer, the brook being lost to sight and sound, unless you are right upon it.*[399]

A description from *Forest and Stream* magazine in 1914 captured exactly what visitors might see:

> *The flume is a sight worth going miles to see and in winter it has a charm never dreamed of by its summer visitors....The little river was buried deep under several feet of snow, and the south side of the flume was one great glittering mass of icicles. The melting snow and ground water that continually trickles from the top of the ledges, freezes as it runs down and forms these icicles which hang from the top of the ledges and reach to the snow.*[400]

In 1922, photographer Kenneth Dudley Smith encouraged prospective wintertime visitors with advice on what to wear and what photographic items to carry. In the early 1920s, Smith himself had gone to see the Flume where "enormous icicles, forty feet in length, colored in white, light green and yellow made the place truly a fairyland."[401] Reverend H.J. Foote in his April 1924 description of "The Flume in Winter" in the *Granite Monthly* similarly extolled the virtues of a wintertime visit, a trek

WINTER IN THE FLUME
FRANCONIA NOTCH, N.H

Right: Wilson Pote. *Line of Snowshoers Headed to the Flume*, photograph, 1924. *Courtesy of the Upper Pemigewasset Historical Society.*

Opposite: Bromley & Co. *Winter in the Flume, Franconia Notch, N.H.*, real photo postcard, circa 1920. *Author's collection.*

he estimated that only about some one hundred individuals had made up to that time.[402] Further popularizing the Flume during this season was a party of newsreel men who made their way into Franconia Notch in winter 1928 to document photographically the wonders that had helped inspire a $400,000 fundraising campaign. Though one of the men broke through the ice on Flume Brook, the group was nonplussed given the beauty surrounding them.[403] As indicated by this accident, however, winter in the Flume was potentially hazardous, and Smith mentions the leader of his own expedition, who "with more courage than brains" plunged into the Pool after approaching the edge on skis.[404]

Despite the difficulty and potential dangers, increasingly more ventured out in the 1930s to see the Flume in winter, encouraged by the journalism noted above.[405] The lure became virtually irresistible once the society began to encourage use of the Flume Reservation as a sports venue. For a brief period, the Flume was the focus of winter recreation in Franconia

A Winter Hike in the Flume, photograph, circa 1923. *Courtesy of the Upper Pemigewasset Historical Society.*

A Woman on Snowshoes in the Flume Gorge, Franconia Notch, N.H., on a Clear Winter Day, glass lantern slide, 1929. *Courtesy of the Appalachian Mountain Club Library & Archives.*

Notch, a development coinciding with the first regular plowing of the notch road (1927) and one immediately predating the development of Cannon Mountain as a skiing center.[406]

Within the Flume Reservation, a former tote road running from the top of the Flume south toward Ed Clark's Eskimo Dog Ranch (now Clark's Trading Post) and North Woodstock was developed as the Flume Ski Trail, while the reservation paths provided additional trails for novice skiers.[407] A snowshoe trail followed the east bank of the Pemigewasset and linked the Flume Covered Bridge with the ski trail one and a half miles below.

Beginning in 1931, the Boston & Maine Railroad operated "snow trains," which conveyed winter sports enthusiasts to the region. The final snow train of the 1931 season was typical, with three trains conveying 1,274 visitors to Franconia Notch in the midst of a snowstorm. "The Flume with its giant icicles also drew a throng. With courteous members of the local women's committee acting as 'check girls,' young and old left their equipment at the entrance, and began to climb through the magnificent spectacle of the giant frozen falls and ripples. Some of the more adventuresome took their skis along and enjoyed the thrill of sliding down the Flume." A sugar-on-snow party at Charkarohen Sugar House and opportunities to drive or be driven by Clark's Eskimo dogs added to the merriment.[408] In 1933, the Forest Society accommodated skiers by providing straw-filled trucks to convey them to the Flume, where they were admitted free of charge. A series of separate trains on February 4 brought 3,081 to New Hampshire for the day, of whom "more than 2000 enthusiasts were carried in trucks to the gates of the Flume Reservation where they tramped, skied or snowshoed up through the Flume, with its great icicles and dazzling Winter brilliance."[409]

The great increase in winter visitation to the Flume during the 1930s was remarkable but no longer worthy of note as so many took the opportunity to explore it. "Nor is a winter trip to the Flume on snowshoes a daring feat to be bragged about as it was in 1920," remarked author Ella Shannon Bowles in 1938, "for everyone you meet now has been into the gorge on skis."[410]

DIFFERING VISIONS

The 1938 opening of the Cannon Mountain Aerial Tramway at the opposite end of Franconia Notch accelerated Cannon's development as a winter recreational center and shifted the locus of winter sports there from the Flume. Buoyed by the enthusiastic response that greeted the arrival of the tramway, the Aerial Tramway Commission in September 1941 promoted further commercialization of the northern end of Franconia Notch, proposing bathing in Echo Lake and the construction of a bathhouse there. With its slick brochures and glossy advertising, the development-minded commission was critical of what it considered the Forest Society's low-key, even dowdy approach to management of the Flume Reservation. Though it held no authority over the Flume, the commission nonetheless chided the society, expressing that it "would like to see the entire Flume area taken over and improvements made with a view towards widening the public appeal for that area."[411]

The Forest Society, however, had a different mission, which Ayres was cautious in protecting. When promotional cards for the Flume were printed blaringly bearing the phrase "ALL REVENUE IS USED FOR UPKEEP AND IMPROVEMENT OF THE PROPERTY" prominently at the top, Ayres asked that they be reprinted: "I shouldn't like to have any statement go out from the Society with this item in so conspicuous a position."[412] Promotion was intended to be modest, tasteful and highly professional. When Bodwell

Putnam Photo. *Flume T House, Franconia Notch, N.H.*, real photo postcard, circa 1935. *Author's collection.*

suggested the addition of four scales on which visitors could weigh themselves for a penny in 1934, Ayres was initially skeptical, though he ultimately relented. "I have felt some hesitation about cheapening the tone of our general layout," he remarked.[413]

Both Bodwell and Ayres understood themselves as stewards of the reservation and were careful to foster its protection. The society engaged noted Boston landscape architect Arthur Shurcliff to plan the reforestation of not only the Flume Reservation but all of Franconia Notch, and it supported Shurcliff's approach, which emphasized forest preservation and limited commercial activity. Placards throughout the reservation bore many of Bodwell's aphorism-like admonitions directed at both guests and employees. "Do Not Pick Flowers or Disturb Vegetation," read one. "Others Who Visit the Reservation Can Then Enjoy Its Natural Beauty." In another, Bodwell made clear his expectations of Employees: "EVERY MEMBER OF THE FLUME PERSONNEL IS EXPECTED TO KEEP THE RESERVATION ABSOLUTELY CLEAN. Do not throw down match sticks, cigarette butts, wrappers, or anything on the grounds, in the garage stalls, or in the buildings. I count on YOU to live up to this rule." Even the Flume Reservation Tea House menu reminded, "A careless cigarette or camp-fire may destroy the growth of one hundred years."

The approaches of the tramway commission and Forest Society in fact represented two differing visions regarding the future of Franconia Notch and its natural attractions, one favoring commercialized recreation and the other promoting more passive uses coupled with forest preservation. Reflective of a tension within the modern conservation movement, these two views would ultimately need to be reconciled in order to create a unified vision for Franconia Notch's future.

THE GREAT NEW ENGLAND HURRICANE AND SENTINEL PINE BRIDGE

In 1938, the Flume experienced its most extensive environmental damage to date when the Great New England Hurricane of September 21 destroyed nearly three hundred acres of forest within the reservation. Bodwell estimated that 50 percent of the Flume Reservation's trees had been blown down by extreme and sustained winds. Among the lost trees was the Sentinel Pine. "Across the Pool the Sentinel Pine is felled and the fine virgin stand of pine and red spruce is practically all flat," Bodwell informed Forest Society president Allen Hollis the following day.[414] Although footbridges in the Flume and above the Pool were washed away, the Flume, its walkway and the covered bridge survived.

Damage throughout New Hampshire was widespread. Large-scale efforts to salvage as much down timber as possible were made under the direction of the Northeastern Timber Salvage Administration (NETSA), which was established to address the problem. At the Flume, the Forest Society accomplished its own salvage work, and state and federal forestry officials subsequently cited the Flume Reservation as one of the best post-hurricane cleanup operations in all New England.[415] By January 1939, a section of the Flume ski trail from the top of the Flume to the Daniel Webster Highway near the Hotel Franconia was reopened, with blowdowns cleared by the Civilian Conservation Corps. At the start of the 1939 summer tourist season, Christopher Janus of the *New York Times* looked to put a positive spin on the previous fall's devastation, remarking that scenic views had been improved and much deadwood cleared. Regarding the Flume Reservation, Janus reported that the hurricane had opened extensive views toward the Flume, repeating Eleanor Early's assertion made in the immediate aftermath of the storm that vistas had been opened up between the Flume and Indian Head and near Whitehouse Bridge a mile north of the Flume.[416]

After Hurricane: Flume [Two Young Men Standing beside Flume Brook, Franconia Notch, N.H.], October 1, 1938, photograph, 1938. *Courtesy of the Appalachian Mountain Club Library & Archives.*

The Pool, Franconia Notch, N.H., real photo postcard, circa 1930. *Author's collection.*

The Pool and Sentinel Pine Bridge—Franconia, N.H., real photo postcard, circa 1939. *Author's collection.*

The Forest Society assured visitors at the start of the 1940 season that "so thoroughly has clean-up work progressed that the only noticeable change on the way to the Flume will be the marked increase in overhead light and the abundance of seedlings and sprouts springing up where the larger trees were blown down. Most of the stumps have been cleared or made less noticeable and the main path is in good shape."[417] Nonetheless, the damage sustained was extensive, and work still continued on clearing the vicinity of the Pool.

The Forest Society demonstrated its own commitment to the importance of timber salvage by replacing the bridge above the Pool in 1939 with an entirely new covered structure constructed completely from downed trees, including the iconic Sentinel Pine. Sixty feet of the Sentinel Pine's trunk was drawn by means of horses and a steel cable across the gorge to serve as the pedestrian bridge's carrying beam. Salvaged wood from other fallen trees was hand-hewn for mortised and tenoned framing members, which were joined by wooden pegs. John G. Welch and Joe Poloquin, known as "Indian Joe," produced the shingles to clad the roof. Following its completion, the Sentinel Pine Bridge, situated forty feet above the Pemigewasset River, was termed by a syndicated columnist as "one of the most attractive covered bridges ever erected."[418] Since that time, it has become a noted landmark and has been frequently photographed.

WARTIME FLUME

While the Flume Reservation weathered the environmental disaster of the 1938 hurricane, the advent of war in December 1941 posed a new threat. Business owners in the White Mountains were clearly concerned about the impact possible rationing might have and prior to the war had balked at the suggestion of "gasless Sundays" as a war preparedness measure, perceiving it as a threat not only to their livelihoods but also to the region's $4 million tourist industry.[419]

The first summer of the war, 1942, saw the Flume operating over 80 percent below 1941 levels. Tourists, some guilty about enjoying themselves in the midst of a war, also had difficulty in making the trip that far north once rationing of tires (December 27, 1941) and gasoline (March 15, 1942) was implemented; attractions in southern New Hampshire closest to the center of population in New England fared better.[420] The decline in attendance also impacted restaurants, cabins and motels that relied on the tourist trade, as well as the aerial tramway and the society's Lost River Reservation at Kinsman Notch, which closed following the 1941 season and did not reopen until 1946. For those visitors making it as far north as the Flume, they tended to stay longer, making the most of the limited gasoline available. "This year…instead of 'tourists' they will be 'vacationists' staying for longer periods," rationalized one newspaper advertisement. "You've always saved money for a vacation—why not save gas and rubber too? What's to hinder?…Come early—stay longer—it'll do you good!"[421] Rail and bus schedules made travel feasible for those of limited means or without automobiles.

Beginning in the summer of 1943, some of the region's larger hotels failed to open, in part due to ongoing manpower shortages, but newspapers continued to encourage tourists to visit the White Mountains and the Flume.[422] To accommodate war-weary travelers that year, the Flume extended its season to mid-October for those coming to view the foliage. Virtually none did, and the Flume for the duration of the war remained nearly deserted. The Flume was later described as "practically closed" for the 1943 and 1944 seasons, and Bodwell was not on hand.[423] The Flume buses, famous for transporting passengers from the teahouse to Boulder Cabin, were also absent, having been sold to aid the war effort.

In May 1945, the Flume reopened with reduced services. Guests had to walk to the chasm; fountain and tearoom services were offered on a

Bromley. *Flume Falls, Franconia Notch, N.H.*, real photo postcard, circa 1920. *Author's collection.*

limited basis; and plans were for the Boulder Cabin to remain closed unless otherwise warranted by unexpected attendance. That year, the society also gave up its management of the Profile Shelter or Echo Lake Coffee Shop concessions, operations there being assumed by the State Forestry and Recreation Commission.

CHAPTER 9

"OUR COMMISSION BELIEVES IN THE MIDDLE WAY"

THE STATE PARK YEARS, 1947–2018

POSTWAR COMMERCIALIZATION

Termination of the Forest Society's direct management of the Flume in October 1947 was accompanied by the revival of discussions related to the site's future commercialization. Ironically, while some state authorities had argued prior to the war that the Flume was not enough of a commercial draw, certain residents maintained that the Flume was in fact over-commercialized, much to the detriment of smaller competing businesses in Lincoln and North Woodstock.

As noted earlier, commercialization of the Flume had drawn criticism as early as the 1860s, with renewed critiques in the 1920s and in 1934 when, on December 2 of that year, a town hall meeting attended by over two hundred was held in Carroll in an effort to generate support for legislation preventing the commercialization of state lands. Representative Harry A. Goodwin and other politicians spoke against the commercialization of Franconia Notch. Senator Roberts of Lancaster, while acknowledging the positive work of the Forest Society, argued that commercialization of state lands should not be permitted.[424]

In 1947, a New Hampshire legislative bill that would have earmarked $50,000 for what were deemed critically needed postwar improvements in Franconia Notch State Park revived opposition to the commercial aspects of the Flume operation among some local business owners. Ed Clark,

Avalanche Falls, Flume Gorge, Franconia, N.H., real photo postcard, circa 1920. *Author's collection.*

operator of Clark's Trading Post, contended that it was unfair for the Flume, which he characterized as "a gold mine," to be assessed at a lower tax rate that allowed it to leverage greater purchasing power. Others criticized the provision of non-recreational services such as souvenir stands and snack shops. Clark's wife, Florence, cited the Flume's fifty-cent chicken lunches, which sold at North Woodstock for eighty-five cents, as an example of how the operation undercut local small businesses.[425] The state countered that tourists expected such services and that it was consequently obliged to provide them. Contrarily, some business owners pointed to the volume their own concerns did and attributed it to the state's participation in and encouragement of tourism, then New Hampshire's second-largest industry. The debate raised the issue of just how deeply involved the state should be in funding commercialized recreation, a discussion that continues today.

FRANCONIA NOTCH FOREST RESERVATION AND STATE PARK

The Forest Society, soon to be out of the business of managing the Flume, avoided being drawn into the fray regarding Franconia Notch's commercial future. Under the 1928 agreement, Governor Charles M. Dale took title to the Flume Reservation on behalf of the state on October 3, 1947.[426] "Here New Hampshire preserves for the world the best she has in scenic beauty, symbol of her hospitality and her offer of inspiration," he remarked as part of ceremonies that included the dedication of a memorial tablet to Ayres at Echo Lake and commemoration of twenty years of stewardship of the Flume Reservation by the Forest Society.[427] Responsibility for the former reservation was delegated to the New Hampshire Forestry and Recreation Commission, which operated the other attractions at Franconia Notch with the exception of the aerial tramway.

The Forest Society, like the Abbotts before it, had recognized the revenue-generating possibilities of the Flume. Forest Society secretary Edgar C. Hirst informed the assembled crowd at the October ceremony that "the earning power of the Flume Reservation has proved to be high. The potentials for further development and improvements from its earnings are here."[428] Yet Hirst cautioned the state against the temptation toward excessive monetization of the Flume, citing the society's own experience over the course of twenty years. "The incentive existed for profit as a

Putnam Photo. *The Flume, Franconia Notch, N.H.*, real photo postcard, circa 1920. *Author's collection.*

means of making much needed repairs and improvements. But we have tried not to let our desire for net income weigh too heavily, striving to keep standards of service and maintenance high and prices reasonable; because we believed our subscribers and the people of the state would wish to have it so." Arthur Shurcliff had offered similar advice in 1941: "Any effort to make a concession or a utility a source of income beyond the normal and relatively small requirements of visitors, would jeopardize the very purpose for which the Notch was acquired, and would threaten public confidence in the custody of the State."[429]

The warnings went unheeded. Immediately following Hirst's address, W.R. Brown, chairman of the New Hampshire Forestry and Recreation Commission, spoke and praised the Flume's envisioned role subsidizing New Hampshire's growing state park system. "From an economic standpoint, the securing of the income from the Flume by the state…will create opportunity for expansion in the Notch and elsewhere."[430] Ironically, Brown's remarks appeared to corroborate the 1928 *Milford Cabinet* editorial that had suggested that the state was less keen on preserving the Notch and more intent upon securing the Flume's revenue.

Regarding the matter of balancing commercial and recreational interests with those of wilderness preservation, Brown felt confident that the state could achieve this, and his statement is worth quoting in full, as it laid out the state's philosophy regarding its scenic attractions:

> *As to the general policy of operation of Franconia Notch Area, there appear to be two conflicting view*[s] *that have received publicity. From the ultra conservative standpoint, the scenic splendor of this popular area should be preserved as a sylvan wilderness, where only quiet and solitude should prevail and the minimum provision made for the public. From the other extreme standpoint this area should be developed with a view towards receiving the greatest revenue for the greatest number of people even at the expense of some of its natural wildness. Our Commission believes in the middle way between these extremes, signified by the expression, "Use but not Abuse." It is confident that Franconia Notch's wilderness splendor can be preserved by the careful protection of its natural scenery, and at the same time, by good planning, the comfort of the myriads of nature lovers who will pour through this notch can be provided for.*[431]

The ultimate name the area would adopt, Franconia Notch Forest Reservation and State Park, reflected this duality of purpose and the seeming reconciliation of development- and conservation-minded visions. The Flume was to be saved from despoliation but was to be promoted for use, a tricky balancing act at the heart of the modern environmental movement.

THE GOLDEN AGE OF AUTO TOURISM

Esso. *New England Road Map with Pictorial Guide*, 1951. *Author's collection.*

In 1874, Mr. Lancaster, a character in Percy Curtiss's novel *Sloppy Dingle*, remarked of the Flume, "The quiet is so deep, the free air, the heavy trees, the sunshine, all so full and certain and fixed, one could be sure of finding the same a hundred years from now."[432] And so it could. Few changes were made at the Flume by its new managers, the Forestry and Recreation Commission, and the tourist experience in 1947 differed little from that of Curtiss's day aside from an increase in admission to fifty cents.

Post–World War II economic growth brought with it a burgeoning middle class with increased leisure time and newly acquired automobiles resulting in an upsurge in tourism. By 1948, 85 percent of tourists were arriving in the White Mountains by automobile, and the 1950s marked the height of family vacation and holiday road trips from which the Flume benefited.[433] Construction of new roadways like the Everett and Spaulding Turnpikes in southern New Hampshire improved accessibility to the Flume and reduced the time needed to reach it. Visits were also made more enticing by the boom in motel construction along the Daniel Webster Highway in North Lincoln as modern accommodations began to supplement the 1930s-era cabins that ranged in price from two to five dollars a night. Meanwhile, large regional resort hotels dating from the previous century, now struggling financially in the face of changes in how Americans traveled, looked to new ways to attract guests. During the 1947 season, the Twin Mountain House at Carroll offered seven-day vacation packages including accommodation and free admission to several attractions, including the Flume, for seventy-five dollars per person, hoping to tempt guests to stay for more than a night.[434] Shady wayside stops on the route to the Flume like the Fay Wayside Area in North Woodstock outfitted with picnic tables allowed motorists to stop to enjoy inexpensive packed lunches. Numerous guides aimed at the motoring public provided tips, suggested itineraries and rated accommodations for prospective tourists.

For those not wishing to drive, package tours in the form of bus touring with visits to the Flume also remained popular and easy. Travel writers such as the *New York Times*'s Mitchell Goodman promoted bus lines like Greyhound and Trailways with their modern conveniences, including observation decks, skylights, air conditioning and restrooms, in contrast to buses a generation earlier that were stuffy with uncomfortable seating.[435]

Another dramatic change was the aggressive marketing of the Flume through state-issued brochures and publications by regional marketing associations like the White Mountains Region Association. While earlier publications by the Forest Society had been designed primarily as souvenirs that were offered for sale at the time tourists visited and served only a secondary marketing purpose, in the postwar era, potential visitors were targeted with stylish brochures advertising the Flume and the region's other attractions, as well as providing information on roads and accommodations in an effort to draw new visitors. Increasingly, the Flume was featured in postwar magazines and travel journals, including *New Hampshire Profiles*, which included glossy full-color images and folksy writing that appealed to readers and encouraged them to visit.[436] The Flume Covered Bridge with Mount Liberty looming in the background, while previously featured on numerous picture postcards, emerged during this era as a uniquely identifiable New Hampshire image, and it was used to

New Hampshire Profiles 13, no. 6 (June 1964), cover. *Author's collection.*

brand everything from calendars and jigsaw puzzles to highway maps and telephone books. The result was a booming tourist industry, with the Flume witnessing heavy visitation when New Hampshire logged five consecutive record-breaking years during the mid-1950s.[437]

HIGHWAY DEVELOPMENT THREATENS THE FLUME

Increased postwar visitation at the Flume and other White Mountains attractions created a demand for new and better roadways. While Franconia Notch had been threatened by lumber interests that had sought to exploit the resources of the region at the expense of tourism during the first quarter of the century, controversial highway development posed a similar threat to the Flume and the surrounding area in the mid-twentieth century. As early as 1938, the *New York Times* had perceived the shared attitudes of the lumber industry and road builders toward forest preservation when an article noted, "'Everybody' wants to spare the tree now except the lumberman and the wideners of roads for the inexorable automobile."[438]

The road between the Flume and Profile Houses, incorporated since 1922 as part of the Daniel Webster Highway, at one time had been considered one of the best and most scenic in the region. By 1924, however, the portion of the highway passing through Franconia Notch was characterized as "more of a race course for automobiles than a route of pleasure."[439] Despite this characterization, speeding along the highway during the peak summer season was impossible, as the appeal of the Flume as well as Franconia Notch's scenery and other attractions choked the road with automobiles. "The stream of automobiles is so great," noted one mid-1920s observer, "that on holidays the narrow band is unable to accommodate them and hundreds are unable to press through."[440] In midsummer 1926, hot weather drove hundreds to the mountains, where "motor traffic had never before been so heavy," much of it a result of the Daniel Webster Highway's designation as Route 3 that same year.[441]

In 1930, tentative plans for a dual highway through the notch were drafted in order to relieve congestion and improve traffic flow. The proposal called for a roadway running on the west side of the Pemigewasset River nearly parallel with the existing roadway from Indian Head to Echo Lake. Construction, however, was ultimately postponed by the worsening economic depression and the subsequent war.

Improvements to the Franconia Notch highway (control of which had passed to the state highway department in 1940) were revived when, in 1956, the Interstate Highway Commission ordered a study for a route between Plymouth and Littleton. It was not until release of its study two years later that opposition to the proposal for a four-lane highway through Franconia Notch, later designated as Interstate 93, emerged.[442] In 1958, state recreation director Russell B. Tobey claimed a highway through the notch would destroy its scenery as well as the recreational value of the Flume and other features, and he suggested that an alternate route to the west of the Kinsman Range be reconsidered. Threatened reduction of the federal construction subsidy from 90 to 50 percent for a highway routed around Franconia Notch, however, prompted New Hampshire legislators to conclude that such a course would be both impractical and fiscally irresponsible.

At issue was the eight-mile stretch through Franconia Notch. Conservationists and preservationists feared the environmental damage it would do to the notch, as well as the potential threat it posed in destabilizing the famous Old Man of the Mountain. Drawing upon the rich cultural history of Franconia Notch that included the Flume, one opponent stressed, "This is our heritage." Proponents countered that the highway, to be designated as Interstate 93, would foster badly needed economic development within the region.[443]

For years, discussions, proposals and counter-proposals delayed a decision. Amendment of the 1973 federal highway bill by Republican senator Norris Cotton of New Hampshire to permit construction of a "parkway" through the notch was ultimately opposed by conservation organizations, including the Appalachian Mountain Club and Society for the Protection of New Hampshire Forests. Despite federal approval for the four-lane highway, the Environmental Protection Agency successfully delayed the project, arguing that it would generate an inordinate amount of traffic that otherwise would not exist. Transportation secretary John A. Volpe added his voice of skepticism regarding the proposal when he declared Franconia Notch "one of the scenic treasures of New England" and indefinitely postponed the project.[444]

Approval by the New Hampshire Highway Department in mid-1974 of the section between Littleton and St. Johnsbury, Vermont, however, made a route through Franconia Notch inevitable. Critics who argued against such segmentation as a political tactic were ultimately successful in the state's abandonment of plans for a four-lane "highway" in favor of a two-lane limited access "parkway" through the northernmost end of Franconia Notch in 1978. The new proposal was accompanied by a New Hampshire Highway Department commitment "that this parkway is the road of the future. It is agreed that there will be no additional lanes or major construction within the park."[445] Work on the finalized parkway would not be completed until 1988.[446] Franconia Notch Parkway is the sole two-lane freeway remaining as part of the United States Interstate Highway System.

MITIGATION

The Flume remained a central concern during the development of I-93 as the highway's proposed path was routed directly through the existing Flume facilities, which by the 1970s were considered outdated. Following World War II, visitation at New Hampshire's state parks had increased exponentially from 250,000 in 1935 to 4 million by the mid-1970s. Usage of Franconia Notch State Park had increased 5 percent annually between 1958 and 1966.[447] The Flume during the mid-twentieth century experienced a corresponding increase in visitors, whose numbers exceeded 235,000 in most years during the early 1970s, resulting in a facility that was worn out and overtaxed. The contemporaneous surge in the popularity of hiking resulted in the heavy usage of existing trails at the Flume and elsewhere in Franconia Notch. The Hidden Spring Nature Trail was cut in 1971 around Breeding Pond, and additional trails at the Flume were considered at the time, in part to relieve congestion.[448] Motorists coming to visit the Flume were unable to find parking places so parked on the side of the road and in other undesignated areas, creating not only a public safety hazard but also potential environmental damage.

Given these infrastructural limitations, the New Hampshire Highway Department in 1979 unsurprisingly found that the facilities at the Flume were approaching their carrying capacity, particularly on August Sundays, and determined that they would reach peak by 1995. While the department recognized that the capacity of the Flume itself was "absolute—only a finite number of people can traverse the boardwalk," it acknowledged that the signage was good and visitors had minimized off-path damage by keeping to designated trails.[449] Additionally, the boardwalk was in good repair, in part due to the practice beginning in 1975 of closing the Flume

Robert Linsdell. *Gilman Visitors' Center*, photograph from Flickr, October 8, 2013.

temporarily during the post–Labor Day lull when water in Flume Brook was low so that experts might rebuild the walk and repair damage due to frost heaves and other disturbances.

The department was also critical of the layout of the Flume's facilities as they existed at the time:

> *Exiting facilities at the Flume present a complex visual and physical situation which is confusing to the park visitor. Maintenance facilities are in such proximity to the public use area that they appear to be part of it. Existing parking facilities are bisected by US Route 3, creating a vehicle/pedestrian hazard further compounded by the tight S-curve alignment and restricted sight distance existing along this section of the highway. The entire setting is now one of a highway environment, rather than a Park environment.*[450]

A design solution calling for new parking, separation of visitor and maintenance facilities and a new interpretation center was recommended. In 1978, the New Hampshire State Historic Preservation Office, headed by George "Gus" Gilman (who also served as the commissioner of the New Hampshire Department of Resources and Economic Development), determined that the buildings that composed the Flume complex were ineligible for listing in the National Register of Historic Places. Proposed for demolition were the former Flume Tea House, the former Flume Clubhouse, the open entrance pavilion dating from 1949, the stagecoach display booth, two garages, a restroom building, two small cabins and a former barn that had been converted to a maintenance shop. Gilman did recommend, however, that the Flume Clubhouse, whose location was within the median strip of the proposed highway, be relocated for use elsewhere in the park.[451]

On July 26, 1985, a $3.2 million visitors' center named for Gilman was dedicated. The center included an information desk, gift shop, cafeteria, ticket office and small auditorium with displays on the area's geology, history and wildlife. Space was also provided to accommodate the restored Concord coach.

CONTINUING CONCERNS

Commercialization of the Flume during the last quarter of the twentieth century continued to be criticized, and the Flume's ability to produce substantial revenue was at times considered to be in conflict with the provision of a meaningful visitor experience.[452] Elsewhere in Franconia Notch, commercialization was encouraged by Commissioner Gilman, who in 1976 called for modernization of the Cannon Mountain Aerial Tramway in order to boost annual proceeds by an estimated $0.25 million. At the Flume, where income was generated largely through entrance receipts, the price of an adult admission rose steadily from $2 to $2.50 (1981), $3 (1982), $4 (1988) and $5 (1989). Revenue from admissions was supplemented by that derived from the gift shop, which became a further object of criticism in 1970 when Gilman proposed limiting the sale of souvenirs in state-operated gift shops to items made in New Hampshire. "It raises the deeper question of the presence of gift shops in state parks, how they serve the basic purpose of the parks and the extent to which any sort of commercial enterprise should be permitted to invade the parks."[453] Some continued to feel that commercialization reflected by souvenir shops like that at the Flume cheapened the visitor experience, while others regarded it as a means to raise significant revenue.

Many visitors were critical of what they considered the Flume's steep admission charge. In 1982, Douglas Rooks, editor of the *Granite State News*, took issue with the three-dollar admission fee, particularly in comparison to the quarter once charged. "There can't be much in maintenance or salary costs involved at the Flume. The admission fee seems to bear no relation to what the state has to spend on it, and has the air, quite simply, of fleecing the tourist. There is something distinctly unpleasant about using a natural wonder for that purpose."[454] While Rooks clearly underestimated the cost involved in operating the Flume, the perception nonetheless remains today of New Hampshire commercializing a natural attraction for gain. In June 2018, a reviewer on Trip Advisor criticized the adult admission cost, which had by then risen to seventeen dollars, and wrote that where "nature has created a beautiful scene, man sees money."[455] Such criticisms harkened back to the mid-1920s, when Karl Abbott had been assailed for his efforts to maximum Flume revenue, and even earlier to the 1860s, when carriages were run from the Profile House in an alleged effort to drive profits.

What modern critics overlook, however, is that since 1991, New Hampshire has been the sole state to require its state park system be self-funded. With approximately two-thirds of New Hampshire parks providing free access and generating no fees, more popular revenue-generating attractions like the Flume have been expected to fund not only themselves but other parks as well. Under this arrangement, New Hampshire's park system ran at a loss for the majority of the nineteen years between 1991 and 2009, during which time a $2.6 million structural deficit was created and the parks faced a crisis when basic maintenance went undone for lack of funds.[456]

The need to generate as much revenue as possible from the Flume in the early 2000s appeared even more urgent following a slump in visitation after the loss of the Old Man of the Mountain in 2003. While many visitors had been drawn to Franconia Notch for the several natural attractions it offered, following 2003, the park had less appeal for many, and visitation at both the Flume and the Cannon Mountain Aerial Tramway suffered accordingly. Between 2002 and 2008, Flume visitation declined nearly 28 percent and hit a low in the latter year when just over 124,000 visited. It was not until 2016 that Flume visitation returned to numbers comparable to those existing prior to 2003.[457]

Since 2010, the park system has turned itself around. In 2014–15, it entirely self-funded its $19 million operational budget by capitalizing on revenue-generating opportunities, including the Flume admission, in order to sustain itself. By 2017, the Flume was the New Hampshire park system's most profitable operation, netting $2,385,397 million in annual revenue.[458] This trend is likely to continue as the Flume prepares to begin year-round operation.

CONCLUSION

For generations, tourists have enjoyed the stunning natural beauty of the Flume. Over time, however, their growing numbers have placed increasing environmental and commercial stress on the site. When New Hampshire assumed control of the Flume Reservation, soon-to-be governor Sherman Adams of Lincoln spoke to the tension inherent in balancing recreation with conservation: "The values in [Franconia Notch] come only from its use. It would not be beautiful if it could not be seen. Its treasures are valueless unless they can be shared by all. The duty of the state is to permit nothing that is beautiful here to be destroyed, nothing to be done that will deface or despoil."[459]

Protecting the natural and cultural heritage of the Flume in the face of increasing visitation has been a concern since the first tourists arrived in the 1830s. These earliest visitors regarded the Flume as a contemplative space that helped them understand their place in the universe and their relationship to God. The influx of curiosity-seeking tourists beginning in the 1850s disrupted this experience and transitioned the Flume from a meditative and introspective space to a heavily patronized social space, increasingly exploited for its commercial value by the Flume House and the later Profile and Flume Hotels Company. Early twentieth-century efforts to extract the maximum profit from the Flume further commodified this natural attraction, while skillful marketing succeeded in drawing ever more visitors to it. Since that time, the Flume has striven to reconcile its remarkable revenue-generating capabilities, necessary for helping subsidize the New Hampshire state park system, with the avowed goal of providing accessibility for all and the demand for ecological preservation—objectives not always in harmony.

The Flume and its relationship to the recreational and commercial future of Franconia Notch, which was designated a National Natural Landmark in 1971, will require care as New Hampshire looks to balance the enjoyment and exploration of nature with the urge to protect it. May it be successful in ensuring that we always have a wild and natural Flume within easy reach of our eyes and feet.

NOTES AND SOURCES

In the absence of a bibliography, full bibliographic references may be found in the notes.

Abbreviations

BDA *Boston Daily Atlas*, Boston, MA
BDE *Brooklyn Daily Eagle*, Brooklyn, NY
BG *Boston Globe*, Boston, MA
DG *Dover Gazette & Strafford Advertiser*, Dover, NH
DN *Derry News*, Derry, NH
FN *Forest Notes*, Society for the Protection of New Hampshire Forests, Concord, NH
GD Grafton County Registry of Deeds, North Haverhill, NH
GMF *Green Mountain Freeman*, Montpelier, VT
HNM *Harper's New Monthly Magazine*, New York, NY
IS *Independent Statesman*, Concord, NH
LDC *Lowell Daily Citizen and News*, Lowell, MA
MU *Manchester Union*, Manchester, NH
NDT *Nashua Daily Telegraph*, Nashua, NH
NE *National Era*, Washington, D.C.
NHS *New Hampshire Statesman*, Concord, NH
NT *Nashua Telegraph*, Nashua, NH
NYEP *New York Evening Post*, New York, NY
NYH *New York Herald*, New York, NY
NYT *New York Times*, New York, NY
PT *Peterborough Transcript*, Peterborough, NH

TC *The Congregationalist*, Boston, MA
UNH Society for the Protection of New Hampshire Forests Collection, Milne Special Collections, Dimond Library, University of New Hampshire, Durham, NH
WME *White Mountain Echo*, Bethlehem, NH

Introduction

1. Euro-centric historians have typically written that the Flume was "discovered" in 1808, but the Abenaki who inhabited the region likely had earlier knowledge of the gorge. The apt description of the Flume as a dream-like vision of nature is by the Editors of Yankee Magazine, *Yankee's New England Adventures: Over 400 Essential Things to See and Do* (Guilford, CT: Globe Pequot Press, 2018), 148.
2. Mason Wade, ed., *The Journals of Francis Parkman*, vol. 1 (New York: Harper & Brothers Publishers, 1947), 20, 21.
3. Frank H. Burt, "The White Mountains Forty Years Ago," *Appalachia* 14, no. 1 (December 1916): 38.
4. Betsy Devine, "Old Man of the Mountain: The Spirit Lives," *NYT*, May 7, 2003, A34.
5. UNH, Box 10, Folder 9, C.T. Bodwell, 1928 Daily Record.

Chapter 1

6. In northern New England, mountain gaps or passes are known as "notches," as they resemble the V-shaped notch made in wood by an axe.
7. Thomas Starr King, *The White Hills: Their Legends, Landscape, and Poetry* (North Conway, NH: Isaac N. Andrews, 1859), 107.
8. "Mountain Views and Coast Scenery, by a Landscape Painter," *Bulletin of the American Art-Union*, no. 8 (November 1850): 130.
9. Charles T. Jackson, *First Annual Report on the Geology of the State of New Hampshire* (Concord: State of New Hampshire, 1841), 97.
10. See C.H. Hitchcock, *The Geology of New Hampshire*, Part II, *Stratigraphical Geology* (Concord: State of New Hampshire, 1877), 158, for an early description of this process. Dr. Laurence M. Gould, geologist of the first Byrd Expedition (1928–30), who made a study of the Flume in 1932, estimated that the fissure in the rocks originated in the pre-Cambrian era.

11. See Starr King, *White Hills*, 127; Hibbard quoted in Guy Roberts, *The Flume and All about It* (Littleton, NH: Littleton Courier, 1923), 2. Roberts writes, "Evidently it is of earthquake origin, lacking as it does evidences of creation by erosion." This theory has since been discredited.
12. Jackson quoted in *NYH*, "The Summer Retreats," July 3, 1853, 6.
13. Jackson, *First Annual Report*, 98. See also Hamilton Child, *Part First: Gazetteer of Grafton County, N.H., 1709–1886* (Syracuse, NY: Hamilton Child, 1886), 13, for a layman's explanation of the formation of the Flume. Today, visitors can view a dike more than a yard in width that occupies the center of the chasm.
14. See Oliver P. Hubbard, "The Condition of Trap Dikes in New Hampshire an Evidence and Measure of Erosion," *American Journal of Science and the Arts* 9, no. 26 (May 1850).
15. See "New England News Summary," *NDT*, August 10, 1869; *NDT*, July 23, 1875, 2; "Howland's Flume," *WME*, July 3, 1880, 1, for a description and image; and "Dixville Notch", *NDT*, July 16, 1873, 1. The *Telegraph* placed the find on Sawyer's River north of Albany and Waterville, but it likely is referring to the flume on Flume Brook, a tributary of the Mad River north of Waterville Valley.
16. Alternate versions record Mrs. Guernsey finding the Flume while searching for a wayward cow by lantern light.
17. Moses Sweetser, *The White Mountains: A Handbook for Travellers* (Boston: James R. Osgood, 1876), 270.
18. Child, *Gazetteer of Grafton County*, 459: "The wife of Jesse Guernsey, of Sugar Hill, now dead, is said to be the first person who ever saw the Flume."
19. Guernsey family genealogists have attributed the find to Olive Guernsey. "In some histories of New Hampshire, 'Aunt Jess Guernsey' is given credit for discovery of 'The Flume' while on a fishing jaunt. Altho[ugh] the age which is assigned her is much older than she actually was, it is likely that 'Aunt Jess' was Olive, wife of Jesse Guernsey." Eva Garnsey Card and Howard Abram Guernsey, *The Garnsey-Guernsey Genealogy* (Urbana, IL: published by the authors, 1963), 145. Based on her own genealogical research, Barbara Avery at the Upper Pemigewasset Historical Society has similarly attributed the discovery to Olive Guernsey [Barbara Avery, "Thoughts and Observations," *Upstream* (Upper Pemigewasset Historical Society) (Spring 2010): 7–9]. It may be that the discovery was attributed to Olive Guernsey when she was age ninety-three, if she survived that long. There is no record of her following 1860.

20. Isaac Hill wrote that "the township of Lincoln in the mountains long contained only a single family keeping a house of entertainment upon the Notch road" but noted that the recent 1840 census had recorded some twenty families resident in the town. Isaac Hill, *The Farmer's Monthly Visitor*, vol. 3 (Concord, NH: John M. Hill, 1841).
21. GD, Book 145, p. 113. In the same deed dated April 6, 1837, Jesse Guernsey is termed "husbandman."
22. Wade, *Journals of Francis Parkman*, 18, 183.
23. Nathaniel Peabody Rogers, *A Collection from the Newspaper Writings of Nathaniel Peabody Rogers* (Concord, NH: John R. French, 1847), 170. Rogers also refers to Guernsey a second time (p. 171) as "the poor benumbed, besotted taverner."
24. Sweetser, *White Mountains*, 270. Among the locations to which he guided tourists was Georgianna Falls. See "Trouting," *The Harvard Advocate* 9, no. 4 (November 25, 1870): 52 for a description of Levi.
25. See Frank O. Carpenter, *Guide Book to the Franconia Notch and the Pemigewasset Valley* (Boston: Alexander Moore, 1898), 102.
26. "Famous Old Huntsman Trapped Last Wolf in N. H.," *NT*, November 28, 1924, 1.
27. Concubar [Daniel P. Connor], *"Old Man Thompson"* (Manchester, NH: Daniel P. Connor, 1911).

Chapter 2

28. *The Fashionable Tour; An Excursion to the Springs, Niagara, Quebec, and through the New England States*, 3rd ed. (Saratoga Springs, NY: G.M. Davison, 1828), 234. For the appropriation, see *Journal of the Senate of the State of New-Hampshire, at Their Session Holden at the Capitol, in Concord, Commencing Wednesday, June 7, 1826* (Concord: State of New Hampshire, 1826), 94, 131, 132, and *Journal of the House of Representatives of the State of New-Hampshire, at Their Session Holden at the Capitol, in Concord, Commencing Wednesday, June 7, 1826* (Concord: State of New Hampshire, 1826), 45, 196, 241–44.
29. Diary, Thomas Cole, October 3, 1828, in Louis Legrand Noble, *The Life and Works of Thomas Cole* (Hensonville, NY: Black Dome Press, 1997), 98.
30. "The Franconia Range," *WME*, August 31, 1878, 2.
31. Frederick W. Kilbourne, *Chronicles of the White Mountains* (Boston: Houghton Mifflin, 1916), 115.

32. Letter, Emerson to Margaret Fuller, September 6, 1839, in Ralph L. Lusk, *The Letters of Ralph Waldo Emerson in Six Volumes*, vol. 2 (New York: Columbia University Press, 1939), 221.
33. Henry David Thoreau, *Walking with Thoreau: A Literary Guide to the Mountains of New England* (Boston: Beacon Press, 2001), 188n.
34. Bradford Torrey, ed., *The Writings of Henry David Thoreau, Journal*, vol. 4 (Boston: Houghton Mifflin, 1906), 302, 303. Elizabeth Hoar was the sister of Edward S. Hoar of Concord, who, like his sister, was interested in botany. Edward Hoar accompanied Thoreau to Maine in 1857.
35. Daniel Denison Slade, "In the White Mountains with Francis Parkman in 1841," *New England Magazine* 11, no. 1 (September 1894): 95.
36. Wade, *Journals of Francis Parkman*, vol. 1, 19, 20.
37. Ibid. Parkman made no mention in a subsequent letter to his father of the difficulties he encountered locating the Flume. Letter, Francis Parkman to Reverend Francis Parkman Sr., July 29, 1841 in Wilbur R. Jacobs, ed., *Letters of Francis Parkman*, vol. 1 (Norman: University of Oklahoma Press, 1960), 8.
38. Slade, "In the White Mountains with Francis Parkman."
39. "A Great Curiosity," *Wisconsin Argus* (Madison, WI), September 4, 1849, 1. The item was reprinted from the *New Hampshire Patriot.*
40. See William M'Leod, "The Summer Tourist.—Scenery of the Franconia Mountains, N.H.," *HNM* 5, no. 25 (June 1852): 4–11; "The White Mountains," *TC*, August 20, 1858.
41. Tempered by Transcendentalism, visitors contemplated nature at the Flume, believing that higher truths would be revealed. The tendency to regard the Flume as a religious manifestation of God's handiwork has continued to the present day. In 1924, Mrs. Ida F. Coons wrote the *Derry News* of "privileges which God [had] extended" to her, including the Flume. "Yesterday, I again stood at the top of a stretch of rock of the east, looking down on a great chasm between, through which flows a great stream of water, 'the flume.' Onward, ever onward, the waters flow—we know not where, lost in the 'Great Deep,' and so it is with each, and everyone of us. 'Onward, ever onward,' we know not where, but to 'Eternity.'" "Reveries," *DN*, September 19, 1924, 7.
42. Nathaniel Peabody Rogers, published in a paper of small circulation October 1, 1841, and quoted in "The Fashion," *NYH*, July 9, 1853, 3.
43. "Visit to the White Mountains…No. III," *New York Daily Tribune*, November 4, 1843, 2.
44. "Mountain Scenery," *The Caledonian* (St. Johnsbury, VT), September 17, 1839, 2.

45. Charles Lanman, *Letters from a Landscape Painter* (Boston: James Munroe, 1845), 128; "A Trip to the White Mountains," *GMF*, September 19, 1865, 1. For his 1856 *Adventures in the Wilds of the United States*, Lanman changed the word "holy" to "shadowy." Charles Lanman, *Adventures in the Wilds of the United States and the British North American Provinces*, vol. 1 (Philadelphia: John W. Moore, 1856), 247; GD, Book 169, p. 64.
46. "The White Hills," *North American Review*, Vol. 90 (January 1860): 253.
47. "Nature," *BDE*, September 29, 1879, 2; "White Mountains," *DG*, September 3, 1853.
48. Eleanor Early, *Behold the White Mountains* (Boston: Little, Brown & Company, 1935), 19. Early is generally unreliable. She, too, writes that the Flume was created by an earthquake.
49. "Letter from the Editor," *NE*, September 2, 1852, 143.
50. "A Trip to the Franconia Mountains," *Vermont Chronicle* (Bellows Falls), August 14, 1869, 4.
51. "Visiting the White Mountains," *GMF*, July 28, 1875, 2.
52. "Editorial Correspondence," *Richmond Enquirer*, September 6, 1852, 1.
53. "Nature," *BDE*, September 29, 1879, 2.
54. "Northern New-England as a Summer Resort," *NHS*, June 26, 1851.
55. "White Mountains," *NYH*, August 20, 1859, 3.
56. Lillian Foster, *Way-Side Glimpses, North and South* (New York: Rudd & Carleton, 1860), 226.
57. "To the White Mountains," *BDA*, August 12, 1850.
58. The railroad coaches were later supplemented by private coaches. For an anecdotal history, see Freeman Willis and Henry Pratt, "An Old Yankee Innkeeper: His Story, New Hampshire," -39, 1938, Manuscript/Mixed Material, Library of Congress.
59. "Correspondence of the Courier," *Boston Courier*, August 12, 1850.
60. Foster, *Way-Side Glimpses*, 225.
61. "Correspondence of the Atlas," *BDA*, August 11, 1852.
62. "White Mountains," *NYH*, August 20, 1859, 3.
63. "Correspondence of the Atlas," *BDA*, August 11, 1852.
64. Henrietta Payne-Westbrook, *The West-brook Drives* (New York: Peter Eckler, Publishers, 1902), 96, and Frances S. Howe, *14,000 Miles: Carriage and Two Women* (privately printed, 1906), 30 passim.
65. See Bryant F. Tolles Jr., *The Grand Resort Hotels of the White Mountains: A Vanishing Architectural Legacy* (Boston: Goodine, 1998), for an outstanding survey of the development of White Mountain hotels during this period.

66. Starr King, *White Hills*, 107. Others preferred Franconia Notch for similar reasons, including a correspondent of the *New York Evening Post* identified only as P.G. who wrote, "I prefer the Franconia Notch to the White Mountain Notch, because, though it is less savage and rugged, it is more romantic and varied." "A Trip to the White Mountains," *NYEP*, August 3, 1852, 3.
67. Blake quoted in H.C. Pearson, "The Warder of the Pass: A Sketch of Franconia," *The Granite Monthly* 21, no. 3 (September 1896): 151.
68. Harriet Martineau, *Retrospect of Western Travel*, vol. 3 (London: Saunders and Otley, 1838), 71.
69. "A Talk with Our Subscribers," *NE*, September 14, 1854, 146.
70. The Guernseys sold the property by deed dated February 18, 1841, to Levi Parker of Lisbon, New Hampshire, and John Rogers and William C. Thompson, both of Plymouth, New Hampshire, who in turn sold the same premises by deed dated February 28, 1842, to Knight [GD, Book 162, p. 386 and Book 169, p. 64]. Knight's tavern is mentioned in Lanman, *Letters from a Landscape Painter*, 130, and *The White Mountain and Winnepissiogee Lake Guide-Book* (Boston: Jordan & Wiley, 1846). Lanman later mentioned Knight's in published works in the 1850s, apparently unaware that the Flume House had replaced it. See Lanman, *Adventures in the Wilds of the United States*, vol. 1, 247.
71. Hamilton Child, *Part First: Gazetteer of Orange County, Vt., 1762–1888* (Syracuse, NY: Hamilton Child, 1888), 319.
72. GD, Book 191, p. 384; Book 194, p. 358; Book 194, p. 405.
73. "The Late Richard Taft," *NDT*, February 15, 1881, 4.
74. *Boston Post*, July 14, 1849 passim. A news item, "All Sorts of Paragraphs," *Boston Post*, July 11, 1849, 2, similarly labels the Flume House as "new."
75. "Mountain Views and Coast Scenery, by a Landscape Painter," *Bulletin of the American Art-Union*, no. 8 (November 1850): 130; *BDA*, August 3, 1850.
76. GD, Book 219, p. 348.
77. John Gath, "Notes on Flume House Register," MS, UNH Box 9, Folder 23.
78. Edward Everett Hale, *Old and New*, 7:5 (May 1873): 508. Site noted for its south-facing views, see "Winslow House," *NHS*, June 7, 1867; "The Franconia Mountains in May," *IS*, June 2, 1881.
79. Starr King, *White Hills*, 127.
80. Figures from "The Summer Retreats," *NYH*, July 3, 1853, 6; "To Summer Tourists" [Flume House broadside], June 25, 1852, in the collections of the Boston Athenaeum.

81. This opinion dating from 1852 was printed in "The White Mountains," *TC*, September 6, 1883.
82. "Letter from the Editor," *NE*, September 2, 1852, 143. A correspondent to the *New York Herald* deemed it a "superior establishment, both in its structure and all its appointments" ["The New England Retreats," *NYH*, July 18, 1851, 7]. The *Boston Daily Atlas* also termed the Flume House "superior" [*BDA*, August 11, 1852].
83. "White Mountains," *DG*, September 3, 1853.
84. "Editorial Correspondence," *LDC*, July 14, 1858. Many visitors made note of the elephant act, including Amelia M. Murray, *Letters from the United States, Cuba and Canada*, vol. 1 (London: John W. Parker and Son, 1856), 65.
85. "A Talk with Our Subscribers," *NE*, September 14, 1854, 146.
86. Gath, "Notes on Flume House Register."
87. *Daily Dispatch* [Richmond], July 25, 1859, 4. As early as 1854, the *New York Evening Post* declared the Profile House "more spacious and magnificent" than the Flume House ["Our New Hampshire Correspondence," *NYEP*, July 14, 1954, 2]. The *Lowell Daily Citizen* reported, "The Flume House is only surpassed by the Profile; it is not quite so elegant and extensive as the latter but is a right comfortable well-kept retreat" ["Editorial Correspondence," *LDC*, July 14, 1858]. By 1885, the Flume House had clearly slipped from fashion, the *Boston Globe* noting that it was favored by those "who like solid comfort better than style" ["At the Mountains," *BG*, July 5, 1885, 13].
88. "Northern New-England as a Summer Resort," *NHS*, June 26, 1851.
89. "A Talk with Our Subscribers," *NE*, September 14, 1854, 146.
90. "To the White Mountains," *BDA*, August 12, 1850. Lady Amelia Murray praised the "bowling-alleys under cover, where ladies and gentlemen can take exercise and amusement in wet weather." A third alley may have been added by the time Lady Murray visited in 1856, as she mentions "three alleys, and slides for the return of balls" [Murray, *Letters from the United States*, 65].
91. "The White Mountains," *TC*, August 20, 1858.
92. "The Fashion," *NYH*, July 9, 1853, 3.
93. "Correspondence of the Transcript," *Boston Evening Transcript*, July 20, 1854.
94. *New Hampshire Democrat* quoted in "The White Mountains," *Daily Union* (Washington, D.C.), August 26, 1855, 3. These falls along Cascade Brook, which include what is sometimes referred to as the "Baby Flume," may be visited by means of the Basin Cascade Trail.

95. "The Geological Survey," *NDT*, August 24, 1871, 1, for the discovery of Lonesome Lake and "New Hampshire," *NDT*, June 25, 1886, 1, for Bridal Veil Falls.
96. Murray, *Letters from the United States*, 65, 66.
97. "A Talk with Our Subscribers," *NE*, September 14, 1854, 146. Much correspondence to the newspapers of the era from White Mountains tourists reflected this trend. See "White Mountains," *DG*, September 3, 1853, for an example.
98. Robert F. Lucid, *The Journal of Richard Henry Dana, Jr.*, vol. 2 (Cambridge, MA: Belknap Press of Harvard University Press, 1968), 645.
99. "Editorial Correspondence," *Daily Herald* (Cleveland, OH), September 12, 1859.
100. "Our New Hampshire Correspondence," *NYEP*, July 14, 1854, 2. The article gives a fine description of the entertainments and staff at the hotel.
101. "Life at the Watering Places," *Chicago Tribune*, September 18, 1867, 2.

Chapter 3

102. Rogers quoted in "The Fashion." The precipitous drop is today the hill that leads down to the Flume Covered Bridge.
103. Jackson, *First Annual Report*, 12; *Guide to the White Mountains and Lakes of New-Hampshire with Minute & Accurate Descriptions of the Scenery and Objects of Interest on the Route* (Concord, NH: Tripp & Morril, 1850), 39, repeats Jackson's advice nearly verbatim.
104. French quoted in Donald B. Cole, "The White Mountains in 1845: From the Journal of Benjamin Brown French," *Historical New Hampshire* 44, no. 4 (Winter 1989): 218.
105. Paul M. DesAutels, www.ancestry.com/mediaui-viewer/tree/13244023/person/-101721552/media/4981338d-23b8-4243-95be-f153255cebba?_phsrc=RTy1681&_phstart=successSource (accessed July 7, 2018).
106. The carriage road is mentioned as early as August 1850. See "To the White Mountains," *BDA*, August 12, 1850. Starr King in 1859 describes the road similarly and as winding.
107. "The Summer Retreats," *NYH*, July 3, 1853, 6.
108. *Boston Transcript* quoted in "Swimming," *BDA*, August 16, 1856.
109. "The White Mountains," *TC*, August 20, 1858.
110. "Letters from the White Hills, No. 2," *Contoocook Transcript* (Peterborough, NH), July 2, 1852, 2.

111. Starr King, *White Hills*, 127.
112. "Editorial Correspondence," *Daily Herald* (Cleveland, OH), September 12, 1859.
113. Rogers quoted in "The Fashion".
114. Payne-Westbrook, *West-brook Drives*, 97.
115. French quoted in Cole, "White Mountains in 1845," 220, 221.
116. "Items," *LDC*, August 27, 1856.
117. "A First Visit to the American Alps," *Boston Evening Transcript*, September 22, 1882, 2.
118. "A Trip to the White Mountains," *GMF*, September 19, 1865, 1.
119. Frederika Bremer, *The Homes of the New World: Impressions of America*, vol. 2 (New York: Harper & Brothers, Publishers, 1854), 588.
120. Starr King, *White Hills*, 128.
121. Thoreau, *Walking with Thoreau*, 189n.
122. Percy Curtiss, *Sloppy Dingle* (Boston: Andrew F. Graves, 1874), 267, 268.
123. William B. Swett, *Adventures of a Deaf-Mute* (Marblehead, MA: William B. Swett, 1875), 10.
124. Hitchcock, *Geology of New Hampshire*, part II, 157.
125. Ibid.
126. Starr King, *White Hills*, 124; "Walks in the White Mountains No. 4," *Evening Star* (Washington, D.C.), September 11, 1876, 1: "The spectator underneath involuntarily shrinks away with the idea that even the jar of a foot-tread may serve to detach it."; "A Tramp Through the Mountains," *Daily Intelligencer* (Wheeling, WV), September 10, 1880, 3: "You hesitate more than once before you go under it; but finally rush past on the general principle that if it was going to fall it would have done so before."
127. Franklin Benjamin Gage, "Photography on Wheels," *Humphrey's Journal of Photography, and the Allied Arts and Sciences* 11, no. 7 (August 1, 1859): 97–99.
128. Foster, *Way-Side Glimpses*, 230.
129. "Free Society in the Mountains," *NYT*, August 22, 1855.
130. "The White Mountains: Part III," *HNM*, Vol. 63 (1881): 362. The piece was likely written by Samuel Adams Drake, who repeats the story nearly verbatim in his *The Heart of the White Mountains* published the following year.
131. French quoted in Cole, "White Mountains in 1845," 220.
132. Mary Lesley Ames, ed., *Life and Letters of Peter and Susan Lesley*, vol. 2 (New York: G.P. Putnam's Sons, 1909), 336.
133. "Along the Elbe," *HNM*, 46, no. 274 (March 1873): 499.

134. "Editor's Mail Bag," *NT*, January 23, 1928, 4.
135. Warner quoted in Marcia Schmidt Blaine, *Passing Through: The Allure of the White Mountains* (Plymouth, NH: Museum of the White Mountains, Plymouth State University, 2013), 53.
136. "The Summer Retreats," *NYH*, July 3, 1853, 6: "A dangerous bridge for a timid step" [*Appleton's Illustrated Hand-Book of American Travel*, Part I: *The Eastern and Middle States, and the British Provinces* (New York: D. Appleton, 1857), 100–1]. Tree named as hemlock, see John E, Bradlee, *Pocket Guide to the White Mountains and Lake Winnipiseogee, and Lake Memphramagog, with Maps* (Boston: John E. Bradlee, 1862), 66.
137. Rogers quoted in "The Fashion." Rogers called it "wild and picturesque-looking."
138. The writer continued that "the scene of nature's ancient tragedy needs a human catastrophe to point out the moral and adorn the tale, artistically speaking" ["Nature," *BDE*, September 29, 1879, 2].
139. French quoted in Cole, "White Mountains in 1845," 220.
140. Swett, *Adventures of a Deaf-Mute*, 12.
141. Rogers, *Collection from the Newspaper Writings of Nathaniel Peabody Rogers*, 171.
142. Bremer, *Homes of the New World*, 588.
143. "Editor's Table," *The Knickerbocker* 44, no. 2 (August 1854): 194.
144. "At the Old Homestead," *PT*, August 24, 1861, 2.
145. "The Franconia Range," *WME*, August 31, 1878, 2.
146. "The White Mountains: Part III," *HNM*, vol. 63 (1881), 362.
147. "Summer Letters," *BG*, September 3, 1874, 3.
148. Lanman, *Letters from a Landscape Painter*, 247. Lanman may have been swayed in his opinion by the fact that he caught forty-five trout, including one measuring seventeen inches, in a two-hour span in the Pool.
149. "White Mountains," *DG*, September 3, 1853; Payne-Westbrook, *Westbrook Drives*, 163.
150. "The Summer Retreats," *NYH*, July 3, 1853, 6.
151. "Visiting the White Mountains," *GMF*, July 28, 1875, 2.
152. "To the White Mountains," *BDA*, August 12, 1850.
153. 190 feet, see "Nature," *BDE*, September 29, 1879, 2.
154. Dark green [*Gems of American Scenery, Consisting of Stereoscopic Views among the White Mountains with Descriptive Text* (New York: Harroun & Bierstadt, 1878), 14]; lustrous sea-green ["The White Mountains: Part III," *HNM*, vol. 63 (1881): 362].
155. See Starr King, *White Hills*, 125, who describes it as "a gloomy, natural well in the forest."

156. A writer for the *Brooklyn Daily Eagle* manages to use all of these in the course of one paragraph. "Nature," *BDE*, September 29, 1879, 2.
157. H.C. Pearson, "The Warder of the Pass: A Sketch of Franconia," *The Granite Monthly* 21, no. 3 (September 1896): 153.
158. "Walks in the White Mountains No. 4," *Evening Star* (Washington, D.C.), September 11, 1876, 1.
159. "At the Old Homestead," *PT*, August 24, 1861, 2.
160. "A Summer Experience," *Yale Literary Magazine* 27, no. 2 (November 1862): 66.
161. *New York Express* in "Wonderful Escape," *Weekly National Intelligencer* (Washington, D.C.), August 28, 1852, 1. The following year, the *New York Herald* wrote of the incident, "When taken out he was as cool as an iced cucumber, and it required various internal and external applications to restore the requisite equilibrium of caloric" ["The Summer Retreats," *NYH*, July 3, 1853, 6]. The story was deemed worthy for inclusion in *Appleton's Illustrated Hand-Book of American Travel*, 100–1. The incident also appears in Benjamin G. Willey's *Incidents in White Mountains History* (Boston: Nathaniel Noyes, 1857), 41.
162. "News for Wheelmen," *BG*, September 15, 1895, 23.
163. "John Merrill," *WME*, August 16, 1879, 1. The iron pin that held the lashing ring to which Merrill once tethered his boat is still visible in a rock at the base of the Pool.
164. Curtiss, *Sloppy Dingle*, 274.
165. Frank E. Clark, *Our Vacations: Where to Go, How to Go, and How to Enjoy Them* (Boston: Estes and Lauriat, 1874), 50.
166. See Andrew Griscom, "John Merrill: The Philosopher of the Pool," *Stereo World* 8, no. 4 (September/October 1981): 12–14 for a summary of Merrill's career as recorded stereographically.
167. Samuel S. Kingdon, *Kingdon's Dictionary of the White Mountains and Other New England Resorts* (Boston: Samuel S. Kingdon, 1894), 60.
168. Ibid.
169. Introduced as "Professor," see "Editorial Correspondence," *LDC*, July 14, 1858; John Merrill, *Cosmogony: or Thoughts on Philosophy* (East Canaan, NH: G.F. Kimball, 1860), 8.
170. "A Trip to the White Mountains," *GMF*, September 19, 1865, 1.
171. John Merrill, *Lecture Delivered at the Flume House Parlor Before a Company of Editors, on the System of the Earth's Being Hollow* (Gloucester, MA, 1858) appears to have laid out the foundation of his argument, which was expanded upon more fully in 1860's *Cosmogony*.

172. "Editorial Correspondence," *LDC*, July 14, 1858.
173. "The White Mountains: Part III," *HNM*, vol. 63 (1881): 362.
174. "Nature," *BDE*, September 29, 1879, 2.
175. "Visiting the White Mountains," *GMF*, July 28, 1875, 2.
176. Thoreau, *Walking with Thoreau*, 189n. Henry Morford, *Morford's Short-Trip Guide to America* (New York: Sheldon & Co., 1872), 142, labeled Merrill "a strange madman…who paddled visitors round [the Pool] in a crazy boat."
177. "Our Summer Resorts," *NYH*, August 1, 1869, 8.
178. *Gems of American Scenery*, 14.
179. Samuel Merrill, *A Merrill Memorial: An Account of the Descendants of Nathaniel Merrill, an Early Settler of Newbury, Massachusetts* (Cambridge, MA, 1917–28), 424.
180. "A Summer Experience," *Yale Literary Magazine* 27, no. 2 (November 1862): 67.
181. "Walks in the White Mountains No. 4," *Evening Star* (Washington, D.C.), September 11, 1876, 1.
182. "Summer Letters," *BG*, September 3, 1874, 3; "More Fun than a Goat," *BG*, July 20, 1887, 4. The amount for 1874 was equivalent to the average daily wage of an American worker, according to Department of Labor statistics, which placed the daily wage at $2.30¼. See Carroll D. Wright, ed., *Bulletin of the Department of Labor*, No. 18 (September 1898) (Washington, D.C.: Government Printing Office, 1898), 668.
183. Payne-Westbrook, *West-brook Drives*, 164. As measured in terms of relative income, which measures the economic or prestige value of a certain wealth relative to GDP, Merrill's 1880 wealth would equate to approximately $3.4 million in 2018.
184. "Editorial Correspondence," *Daily Herald* (Cleveland, OH), September 12, 1859. "The Pool," *WME*, July 17, 1897, 1, similarly contended that Merrill's peculiarities "were assumed for their ready money value in extracting coin from sympathetic pockets."

Chapter 4

185. Christopher Johnson, *This Grand and Magnificent Place: The Wilderness Heritage of the White Mountains* (Durham: University of New Hampshire Press, 2006), 3. "To the White Mountains," *BDA*, August 12, 1850: "We… would recommend no traveller to leave the White Mountains without

seeing both the Pool and the Flume." In 1891, Colonel C.H. Greenleaf, then owner of the Flume and proprietor of the Flume and Profile Houses, termed the Flume "the object of a pilgrimage to every White Mountain tourist" [Greenleaf quoted in George H. Haynes, *Souvenir of New England's Great Resorts*, 2nd ed. (New York: Moss Engraving Company, 1891)].

186. "A Trip to the White Mountains," *NYEP*, August 3, 1852, 3, considered the attractions the region's mountaintops, Franconia Notch and the Flume. "Summer Resorts," *NHS*, July 28, 1860, considered the Flume "the most surprising curiosity of the whole mountain country."
187. "Five Days Away from Boston," *BDA*, August 29, 1855.
188. "President Grant's Breakneck Ride," *BG*, September 5, 1937, C6.
189. *Summer Saunterings by the B. and L.* (Boston: Boston & Lowell Railroad, 1886), 90.
190. W.C. Prime, *I Go A-Fishing* (New York: Harper & Brothers, 1873), 213.
191. Bremer, *Homes of the New World*, 586–87.
192. Starr King, *White Hills*, 124.
193. *Keyes' Hand-book of Northern Pleasure Travel: To the White and Franconia Mountains, the Northern Lakes and Rivers, Montreal, Quebec, and the St. Lawrence and Saguenay Rivers* (Boston: George L. Keyes, 1874), 92; "The Flume Reservation, Franconia Notch, Lost River" (Franconia, NH: The Flume Reservation, 1937). The recommendation to visit in the morning has frequently been repeated by guidebook authors [see Ray I. Haskell, *What I Know about Mount Agassiz, Bethlehem and the White Mountains* (n.p.: Ray I. Haskell, 1914), 28].
194. "Correspondence of the Atlas," *BDA*, August 11, 1852. "The White Mountains," *TC*, August 20, 1858, agreed, including the Flume as an attraction "one needs to see and see again."
195. See *WME*, July 19, 1879, 3 for an example.
196. "Free Society in the Mountains," *NYT*, August 22, 1855.
197. *The Crayon* 2 (1855): 2.
198. "From the Boys on the Mountains," *LDC*, August 13, 1859.
199. Wolcott quoted in Nancy Osgood, "Josiah Wolcott: Artist and Associationist," *Old-Time New England* 76, no. 264 (Spring/Summer 1998).
200. "Sketchings," *The Crayon* 4, no. 12 (December 1857): 379.
201. "Work of Ralph A. Blakelock," *Brush and Pencil* 9, no. 5 (February 1902): 257–69.
202. Robert L. McGrath, *Gods in Granite: The Art of the White Mountains of New Hampshire* (Syracuse, NY: Syracuse University Press, 2001), 137. The *New York Times* reported that there was "quite a history" attached to the

painting, which was initially sketched during Blakelock's 1877 wedding tour. "Being hard pressed for money," Blakelock promised the painting to a buyer in Rhode Island, but Senator Frederick G. Gibbs learned of the painting and purchased it and was said to have treasured it highly ["F.S. Gibbs's Art Collection," *NYT*, March 17, 1901, 18].

203. McGrath, *Gods in Granite*, 137, 139. Hill maintained a studio at the Flume House.

204. Harry Hibbard, "Franconia Mountain Notch," *Democratic Review* reprinted in "Poetry," *Vermont Patriot & State Gazette* (Montpelier), August 17, 1855.

205. Edward Waldo Emerson and Waldo Emerson Forbes, eds., *Journals of Ralph Waldo Emerson with Annotations*, vol. 6 (Boston: Houghton Mifflin, 1911), 383.

206. Letter, Ellen Tucker Emerson to Edith Emerson, July 2, 1875, in Edith E.W. Gregg, ed., *The Letters of Ellen Tucker Emerson*, vol. 2 (Kent, OH: Kent State University Press, 1982), 178, 179.

207. Daniel Dulany Addison, *Lucy Larcom: Life, Letter and Diaries* (Boston: Houghton Mifflin, 1895), 169.

208. "The White Hills in October," *Continental Monthly*, vol. 2 (1862): 434.

209. For ornithologists at the Flume, see "Bird-Gazing in the White Mountains," *Atlantic Monthly*, 54, no. 121 (July 1884): 54.

210. Letter, Emerson to Margaret Fuller, September 6, 1839, in Lusk, *Letters of Ralph Waldo Emerson*, vol. 2, 221.

211. Frank S. Collins, "Algae of the Flume," *Rhodora* 6, no. 72 (December 1904): 229.

212. See William Gilson Farlow, "Algae of the Flume," *Appalachia*, vol. 3 (1904): 232. Since Farlow, many similar botanical investigations have been undertaken in the Flume. See Annie Lorenz, "Report on the Hepaticae of Franconia Mountains, N.H.," *Bryologist* 11, no. 6 (November 1908): 112, and Janice M. Glime, "Bryophytes of the Flume, Franconia Notch State Park, N.H.," *Rhodora*, 84, no. 837 (January 1982): 149–52 for examples.

213. *Catalogue of American Scenery and Architecture* (Boston: Soule Photograph Company, 1899).

214. Gage, "Photography on Wheels," 97–99.

215. "A Trip to the White Mountains," *Buffalo Express*, August 25, 1862, 1. Fifield died of acute nephritis, though some said he died when the Flume boulder fell on him.

216. Curtiss, *Sloppy Dingle*, 268.

217. "A Trip to the White Mountains," *GMF*, September 19, 1865, 1.

218. "Letter from the Old Granite State," *Fort Wayne Morning Gazette*, August 20, 1877.
219. Arthur Hobart, *A Record of the Perambulations of the Pemigewasset Perambulators, by Their Scribe* (Boston: printed for private circulation [by Rockwell & Rollins], 1866), 24.
220. Lloyd Ostendorf, "A New Mary Todd Lincoln Photograph: A Tour of the White Mountains in Summer, 1863," *Illinois Historical Journal* 83, no. 2 (Summer 1990): 109–12.
221. Edward Marshall Messenger, *A Simple Life of Three-Score Ten* (n.p.: Edward Marshall Messenger, 1911), 33.
222. The Miriam and Ira D. Wallach Division of Art, Prints and Photographs: Photography Collection, New York Public Library, *Visitors at the Flume, 1867*.
223. "Local Mention," *NDT*, August 12, 1871, 2.
224. For cost, see "At Franconia," *NDT*, July 21, 1869, 2. See the collections of the New York Public Library for numerous examples of these stereoscopic views. Dated stereoscopic cards attributable to Fifield in the collection span the years from 1864 through 1880, though he likely practiced for a longer period. Fifield was responsible for a number of iconic images from the era, most notably the *Arctic Philosopher and Wife in the Pool, Franconia Mts., N.H.* (1870).
225. See Richard Hamilton, "The Hotel Marketing Phenomenon: Souvenirs, Mementoes, Advertising and Promotional Materials" in *Historic New Hampshire* 50, nos. 1 and 2 (Spring/Summer 1995) [*The Grand Resort Hotels and Tourism in the White Mountains*]: 95–108.
226. "The Franconia Range," *WME*, August 31, 1878, 2.
227. "Echoes of the Week," *WME*, July 27, 1878, 12.
228. Payne-Westbrook, *West-brook Drives*, 161.
229. *NE*, August 24, 1854, 135, passim.
230. *Portland, White-Mountains & Montreal Rail-road Guide* (Portland, ME: Foster, Gerrish, Printers, 1853); "Motoring a Big Feature of White Mountain Summer Life," *New York Tribune*, July 2, 1905.
231. Clark, *Our Vacations*, 52, 53.
232. Swett, *Adventures of a Deaf-Mute*, 11.

Chapter 5

233. "The White Mountains," *Philadelphia Inquirer*, September 22, 1871, 7.

234. "Gossip of the Summer Resorts," *Chicago Tribune*, August 27, 1869, 2.
235. "Editorial Correspondence," *Daily Herald* (Cleveland, OH), September 12, 1859.
236. "Letter from the White Mountains," *BDA*, August 2, 1861; "A Trip to the White Mountains," *Buffalo Express*, August 25, 1862, 1.
237. "A Trip to the White Mountains on Foot," *GMF*, September 5, 1865, 2. Contrary to this claim, the *Boston Daily Atlas* reported that although accommodations were not provided during the period the Flume House was closed, luncheon was ["New Hampshire," *BDA*, January 16, 1871].
238. Swett, *Adventures of a Deaf-Mute*, 42.
239. "The Season at the White Mountains," *NYT*, June 9, 1866.
240. "Grafton County," *IS*, May 29, 1879.
241. "Our Lake and Mountain Resorts," *IS*, June 27, 1878.
242. Samuel Adams Drake, *The Heart of the White Mountains: Their Legend and Scenery* (New York: Harper & Brothers, 1882), 224.
243. "A Grand 'Old Man,'" *Rocky Mountain News* (Denver, CO), August 2, 1891, 2.
244. "Walks in the White Mountains No. 4," *Evening Star* (Washington, D.C.), September 11, 1876, 1.
245. "Autumn Among the White Hills," *NYEP*, October 24, 1885, 5.
246. GD, Book 329, p. 378.
247. Frederic J. Wood, *The Turnpikes of New England and Evolution of the Same through England, Virginia, and Maryland* (Boston: Marshall Jones, 1919), 244.
248. "A Trip to the Mountains and Seashore," *IS*, July 25, 1878.
249. Toll rates were established in the enabling legislation. See Laws of New Hampshire (1871), Chapter XCVII, "An Act to Incorporate the Lincoln Turnpike Company."
250. Payne-Westbrook, *West-brook Drives*, 161.
251. Wood, *Turnpikes of New England*, 244.
252. Sarah N. (Brooks) Welch, *Franconia Notch: History and Guide* (Littleton, NH: Sarah N. Welch, 1952), 7.
253. Richard G. Marshall, *New Hampshire Covered Bridges* (Concord: New Hampshire Department of Transportation, 1994). The 1886 bridge is 50 feet long, 20 feet 9 inches wide with a roadway width of 17 feet 6 inches and a clear span of 41 feet 4 inches.
254. Ibid.
255. Ella Shannon Bowles, *Let Me Show You New Hampshire* (New York: Alfred A. Knopf, 1938), 174.

256. Starr King, *White Hills*, 124.
257. "The White Mountains: Part III," *HNM*, vol. 63 (1881): 362.
258. Letter, J.D. Whitney to W.D. Whitney, September 16, 1883, in Edwin Tenney Brewster, *Life and Letters of Josiah Dwight Whitney* (Boston: Houghton Mifflin, 1909), 361.
259. C.H. Greenleaf, *History of the Old Man of the Mountains and the Flume* (1923).
260. "News, Notes, and Varieties," *Vermont Phoenix* (Brattleboro), July 25, 1857, 2; *Boston Traveller*, quoted in "The Sad Disaster by Lightning at the White Mountains," *NE*, July 30, 1857, 123; "The Disaster at the Flume House," *NYT*, July 22, 1857, 5.
261. "A Terrific Storm," *BG*, July 8, 1883, 10. Langton was a regular summer visitor to the Flume House, "for years…one of the first to reach and last to leave this famous hostelry" ["Mountain and Shore," *BG*, July 6, 1884, 14]. It is for him that Langton Cascades (now Liberty Cascade) were named. His name is given in various accounts as Laughton, Lancton and Langdon.
262. *Vistas on the C & M. Concord, NH: Passenger Department of the Concord & Montreal Rail Road* (Concord, NH: Concord & Montreal Railroad, n.d.).
263. "The Liberty Cascade," *WME*, August 28, 1897, 1.
264. *NYEP*, July 2, 1883.
265. "A White Mountain Slide," *Hartford Times*, July 12, 1883, 3.
266. Quoted in J.F. Frisbie, *The Franconia Flume: The Causes that Led to Its Formation* (Newton, MA: J.F. Frisbie, 1883), 4.
267. "Hunting a Boulder," *The Times* (Philadelphia), July 22, 1883, 3.
268. Greenleaf, *History of the Old Man of the Mountains and the Flume.*
269. *Daily Herald* [Los Angeles], July 12, 1883, 1.
270. "A Landslide in the Mountains," *Morning Journal and Courier* (New Haven, CT), June 22, 1883, 3.
271. Frisbie, *Franconia Flume*, 8; *Boston Herald* quoted in *Wessington Springs (SD) Herald*, August 4, 1883, 3. The *Boston Globe* wrote that "we look for the old boulder, which so many times has filled us with awe and wonder, with a feeling of longing, as if for an old friend who had left us never to return. How many will share with us this feeling, and come to the old shrine with deep regrets" ["A Terrific Storm," *BG*, July 8, 1883, 10].
272. Howe, *14,000 Miles*, 63.
273. "Editor's Mail Bag," *NT*, January 23, 1928, 4.
274. Warner quoted in Blaine, *Passing Through*, 53.
275. Frisbie, *Franconia Flume*, 7.
276. "Editor's Mail Bag," *NT*, January 23, 1928, 4.

277. Greenleaf, *History of the Old Man of the Mountains and the Flume.*
278. "A White Mountain Slide," *Hartford Times*, July 12, 1883, 3.
279. *NYEP*, July 2, 1883. Current guides distributed to Flume visitors today state that "the boulder has never been found."
280. Charles Dudley Warner, "Their Pilgrimage," *HNM* 73, no. 438 (November 1886): 943.
281. Howe, *14,000 Miles*, 63, 64.
282. "A White Mountain Slide," *Hartford Times*, July 12, 1883, 3.
283. Greenleaf, *History of the Old Man of the Mountains and the Flume.*
284. *Harper's Weekly*, October 28, 1865; *New York Tribune*, May 13, 1876.
285. The law was later codified as part of *The General Statutes of the State of New Hampshire* (1867), Chapter CCLXIII, Section 6: "If any person shall paint the names of any wares or occupation on fences or other private property, or on any rock or natural object, without leave of the owner, he shall be fined ten dollars, one half to the use of the proprietor."
286. Advertisement, *NYT*, April 22, 1865, 8. The path is not identified, and the Crawford Path, Davis Path (which was abandoned about this time) and Fabyan (Ammonoosuc) Path, which was soon afterward succeeded by the cog railway, are all likely candidates.
287. "Archie Hutchington," *HNM* 42, no. 152 (May 1871): 853.
288. Curtiss, *Sloppy Dingle*, 324.
289. "The Gibralters: A Story in Four Letters," *Cazenovia (NY) Republican*, November 8, 1871, 1.
290. Howe, *14,000 Miles*, 147.
291. "A Trip to the Mountains and Seashore," *IS*, July 25, 1878.
292. Ibid.
293. "The White Mountain Excursion," *NDT*, September 16, 1880, 4.
294. *NDT*, advertisements, August 29, 1893, 5, and September 14, 1895, 4.
295. *Raymond's Vacation Excursions: Eighteen Grand Autumn Trips* (Boston: W. Raymond and I.A. Whitcomb, 1888). See also *Raymond's Vacation Excursions. 22: Autumn Trips* (Boston: W. Raymond and I.A. Whitcomb, 1891).
296. Ibid.
297. Ibid., 1882, 60, 62.
298. "White Mountains," *Bangor Daily Whig & Courier*, July 19, 1879.
299. "Away from Home," *North American* (Philadelphia), August 3, 1878.
300. *Littleton Courier* quoted in "Franconia Notch," *WME*, July 12, 1924, 16.
301. "A Trip to the Mountains and Seashore," *IS*, July 25, 1878; "White Mountains," *Bangor Daily Whig & Courier*, July 19, 1879.
302. "The White Mountains," *Chicago Tribune*, September 11, 1868, 2.

303. "Save Franconia Notch," *WME*, August 10, 1878.
304. Lumbermen acquiring tracts in the Flume region at mid-century included Samuel H. Walker of Holderness, New Hampshire, and lumber dealers John Fiske and Nicholas G. Norcross (Fisk & Norcross, Lowell, Massachusetts). See GD.
305. *WME*, July 1, 1893, 5.
306. See the *Transcript*'s editorial in "Flood and Forest," *WME*, July 24, 1897, 20.
307. Harrison quoted in "Save the Forests," *NDT*, November 23, 1892, 3.
308. Francis Parkman, "The Forests of the White Mountains," *Garden and Forest* 1, no. 2 (February 29, 1888): 2.
309. "Pemigewasset Pictures," *WME*, July 23, 1898, 2.
310. New Hampshire Forestry Commission, *Report of the New Hampshire Forestry Commission* (Concord: New Hampshire Forestry Commission, 1897), 156.
311. Ibid.
312. "Timber Owners Busy," *NT*, December 17, 1906, 2. Johnson wound up operations in 1915.

Chapter 6

313. "Fall Excursion to the White Mountains," *Derry Times*, September 14, 1901, 3, and "Among the White Mountains," *Derry Times*, August 5, 1898, 5.
314. *WME*, July 16, 1904, 20.
315. "Motoring a Big Feature of White Mountain Summer Life," *New York Tribune*, July 2, 1905; "White Mountain Visitors," *NYT*, August 18, 1913. See also "Up in the White Mountains/Motorists Out in Large Numbers," *NYT*, September 2, 1914.
316. "Alluring Roads in White Mountains," *NYT*, July 13, 1913, X10.
317. "How to Tour for a Week in the Mountains," *NYT*, August 16, 1913.
318. L.H. Baker, *The Favorite Motorways of New England: Historical and Descriptive* (New York: Henry MacNair, 1915).
319. *Deluxe Hotels of New England* (Boston: C.B. Webster, 1914).
320. "Visitors Flock to White Mountains," *New York Sun*, July 11, 1915, 6:3.
321. "Echoes of the Week," *WME*, August 4, 1900, 15.
322. "For Nature Lovers," *WME*, September 10, 1904, 6.
323. George Golding Kennedy, Journal, 1915–1917, George Golding Kennedy Papers, Archives, Gray Herbarium Library, Harvard University Herbaria:2.

324. Karl Pomeroy Harrington, *Walks and Climbs in the White Mountains* (New Haven, CT: Yale University Press, 1926), 1.
325. See the *BDE*, April 20, 1902, passim for examples.
326. *WME*, July 22, 1899, 3.
327. "Franconia," *WME*, August 28, 1920, 6.
328. A.H. Beardsley, "The Pictorial Wealth of New Hampshire," *Granite Monthly* 54, no. 9 (September 1922): 319, 320.
329. "Wanderin' Around," *Argus-Champion* (Newport, NH), September 3, 1926, 4.
330. "Flume House Burned," *Brattleboro Daily Reformer*, June 28, 1918, 1. Two conflicting accounts of the fire were produced at the time, one stating that the fire occurred before the hotel opened with the entire contents destroyed and a second that the hotel had been opened for two weeks and considerable furniture and contents were able to be salvaged. See *Norwich (CT) Bulletin*, June 28, 1918; *New York Sun*, June 28, 1918, 16; "Flume House Destroyed," *Barre (VT) Daily Times*, June 29, 1918, 8; "Echoettes," *WME*, July 13, 1918, 6.
331. "White Mountains," *BG*, August 31, 1919, 11; "New Tea House at the Flume," *WME*, September 6, 1919, 11.
332. "White Mountains," *BG*, August 31, 1919, 11; "Prediction of Record Breaking Season Comes True in Many New England Resorts," *New York Sun*, July 6, 1919, 4:7.
333. "Franconia," *WME*, August 28, 1920, 6.

Chapter 7

334. Ibid., 11.
335. Karl P. Abbott, *Open for the Season* (Garden City, NY: Doubleday & Company, 1950), 169, 170. The entrance structure was built by contractor Charles Clark of North Woodstock with L. Clarence Miller as foreman. See "Observe 60th Anniversary," *DN*, September 8, 1944, 4.
336. "25 Years Ago in Derry," *DN*, August 17, 1951, 3, and *DN*, May 28, 1953, 2. Toll keeper Chester Merrill of Hudson, New Hampshire, collected $55.03 in $0.06 tolls on one Sunday, "the largest single day thus far of the season" ["Franconia Notch Tolls," *Republican Champion* (Newport, NH), August 21, 1919, 2].
337. Abbott, *Open for the Season*, 169.
338. Ibid., 169, 170.

339. Admission numbers from "Franconia Notch," *WME*, July 12, 1924, 16, and Randall H. Bennett, *The White Mountains: Alps of New England* (Charleston, SC: Arcadia Publishing, 2003). Robert P. Bass, "Franconia Notch in Danger," *American Forests and Forest Life Magazine*, May 1925, gives the figure for 1924 as eighty thousand.
340. "Wanderin' Around," *Argus-Champion* (Newport, NH), September 3, 1926, 4.
341. Ibid. The newspaper suggested that overnight camps were the state's fastest-growing industry at the time.
342. Hotels, including the Alpine House at North Woodstock, still advertised their proximity to the Flume as an attraction.
343. "Through Franconia and Kinsman Notches," *WME*, August 8, 1903, 1.
344. "Echoes of the Week," *WME*, August 6, 1904, 4.
345. Justus Conrad, "A New Way of Profiteering," *Plymouth (NH) Record*, August 31, 1922, and Abbott's rebuttal, Karl Abbott, Letter to the Editor, *Plymouth Record*, September 8, 1922, which is discussed in Kimberley A. Jarvis, *Franconia Notch and the Women Who Saved It* (Lebanon, NH: University Press of New England, 2007), 100.
346. "New Hampshire Will Spend Thousands to Boom State," *Republican Champion* (Newport, NH), May 7, 1925, 8.
347. E.E. Woodbury, *Littleton Courier*, quoted in "Franconia Notch," *WME*, July 12, 1924, 16.
348. Ibid.
349. UNH, Box 9, Folder 22, Letter, Karl Abbott to Editor, *Plymouth (NH) Record*, September 8, 1922.
350. Jarvis, *Franconia Notch and the Women Who Saved It*, and "Nature and Identity in the Creation of Franconia Notch: Conservation, Tourism, and Women's Clubs" (UNH doctoral dissertation, 2002), 70; "Saving Franconia Notch." *Portsmouth (NH) Herald*, October 14, 1976, 4.
351. Abbott, *Open for the Season*, 177.
352. *MU*, August 3, 1923.
353. See Laws of 1925, Chapter 101, pp. 122–23, "An Act to Provide for the Acquisition by the State of the Franconia Notch, so called Lying in the Towns of Franconia and Lincoln, as a Forest Reservation and State Park," and the subsequent amendment, Laws of 1927, Chapter 74, p. 91 for the enabling legislation. According to Philip W. Ayres: "The purchase price of $400,000 was arrived at through conferences between W.R. Brown of the State Forestry Commission, J.A. Foster, State Forester, Gov. Huntley N. Spaulding, representing the state, Mr. Allen Hollis, representing the

Society [for the Protection of New Hampshire Forests], and the owners of the Notch, the Profile and Flume Hotel Companies, after careful estimates had been prepared on timber values by the federal forest service. The complete valuation of the notch is based on reasonable capitalization of the revenue received from the Flume, souvenir stands, and other profit-bearing features of the Franconia region" ["Franconia Notch Campaign Progressing," *Argus-Champion* (Newport, NH), "January 19, 1928, 3]. As early as 1888, Charles Sprague Sargent, director of Harvard's Arnold Arboretum, had urged the establishment of a state reservation in the White Mountains.

354. SPNHF mission statement as adopted in 1904.
355. UNH, Box 10, Folder 8, Letter, Bodwell to Ayres, February 17, 1934.
356. "Society for the Protection of N.H. Forests," *DN*, December 2, 1927, 4.
357. "Franconia Notch," *Milford Cabinet*, January 12, 1928, 4.
358. The reservation was composed of land in Lincoln, being Lot 11, Range 6; Lots 9, 10 and 11, Range 7; and Lots 9 and 10, Range 8. See Grafton County Deeds (Profile and Flume Hotels Company to SPNHF, dated June 6, 1928), recorded Book 606, p. 583. According to a June 15, 1928 open letter from Allen Hollis, president of the SPNHF, the Forest Society had expected to assume management of the entire Franconia Notch tract "during the period required for restoration work" but was unable to agree upon terms with the state. See "Report on Franconia Notch Acquisition," *DN*, July 6, 1928, 3.
359. See copies of the agreement in UNH, Box 9, Folder 29. Ayres quoted in "Franconia Notch Campaign Progressing," *Argus-Champion* (Newport, NH), January 19, 1928, 3. Landscape architect Arthur A. Shurcliff of Boston, who had previously been engaged by the SPNHF for the restoration of its Lost River Reservation, was hired to perform similar work at Franconia Notch. The lands not included in the Flume Reservation were on September 15, 1928, formally designated by Governor Spaulding as Franconia Notch Reservation as a memorial for soldiers of all wars in a simple ceremony held at Profile Lake beneath the Old Man of the Mountain. The *New York Times* believed that the creation of the reservation signaled a new regional interest in conservation and proclaimed "New Hampshire's Forests Saved" when the Franconia Notch agreement and a second to protect Waterville Valley were consummated in 1928.
360. The SPNHF would long regard Lost River "as a model tourist attraction." See Malcolm Taylor, SPNHF in *PT* quoted in "N.H. Conservationists Compete for Land," *DN*, November 30, 1972, 15.

Chapter 8

361. UNH, Box 10, Folder 10, Letter, Bodwell to Rathbun, 1935.
362. See UNH, Box 10, Folder 9, C.T. Bodwell, 1928 Daily Record.
363. Ibid.
364. Ibid.
365. "New Paths to Flume," *BG*, July 30, 1933, 34. Flume visitation, however, was only half that of those who viewed the Old Man of the Mountain, which could be done for free.
366. UNH, Box 10, Folder 10, Letter, Bodwell to Rathbun, 1935.
367. UNH, Box 10, Folder 9, C.T. Bodwell, 1928 Daily Record.
368. Jan Whitaker, *Tea at the Blue Lantern: A Social History of the Tea Room Craze in America* (New York: St. Martin's Press, 2002).
369. UNH, Box 9, Folder 27a, undated clipping.
370. UNH, Box 9, Folder 23, Letter, Bodwell to Ayres, December 15, 1933.
371. Thomas Dreier, "Sunny Meadows Farm Philosophy," undated clipping, UNH, Box 9, Folder 19.
372. Ibid.; UNH, Box 9, Folder 23, Letters, Bodwell to Ayres, November 27, 1933, and December 15, 1933.
373. The historic trail system has since been altered, largely due to the construction of the Gilman Visitors' Center. The westernmost portions of the 1930s-era Wildwood Path, Boulder Path and Flume Bus Road have been discontinued.
374. "Human Habitation to Be Removed from Area in Franconia Notch," *MU*, September 8, 1934.
375. UNH, Box 10, Folder 9, C.T. Bodwell, 1928 Daily Record.
376. "New Paths to Flume," *BG*, July 30, 1933, 34.
377. UNH, Box 10, Folder 10, Letter, Bodwell to Lawrence J. Rathbun, 1935.
378. "Mrs. F.D. Visits White Mountains," *BG*, August 17, 1935, 3. She had visited previously in 1933.
379. "New Paths to Flume," *BG*, July 30, 1933, 34.
380. These were probably the "cabins" mentioned in promotional literature of the Ward Lumber Company of Presque Isle, Maine, which advertised in promotional literature the use of its Maine-style logs at the Flume Reservation. "Maine Style Log Cabins," Ward Lumber Co., Presque Isle, Maine. Promotional brochure, 1930s.
381. UNH, Box 10, Folder 9, C T. Bodwell, 1928 Daily Record.

382. *PT*, September 3, 1936, 8; "This Year's Recreation Business," *PT*, September 16, 1937, 2. The 1937 figure is calculated with the Lost River Reservation, which the SPNHF also operated.
383. UNH, Box 10, Folder 9, C.T. Bodwell, 1928 Daily Record.
384. Carpenter, *Guide Book to the Franconia Notch*, 112, gives a nearly identical description of their location, writing, "A few rods below the Pool a side brook joins the Pemigewasset from the east, over several graceful cascades. They are named the Langton Cascades, in memory of a Mr. Langton, for many years a regular summer guest at the Flume House and an earnest lover of nature."
385. UNH, Box 10, Folder 9, C.T. Bodwell, 1928 Daily Record.
386. Ibid.
387. "Great Pine Near Flume," *MU*, September 25, 1934.
388. UNH, Box 10, Folder 10, Letter, Bodwell to Rathbun, May 27, 1936.
389. UNH, Box 9, Folder 23, Letter, Bodwell to Hollis, September 22, 1936.
390. "Last of Old Coachmen Drives Stage to Flume," *BG*, August 25, 1932, 8, states that the stage ran until 1915, when it was replaced by buses.
391. UNH, Box 9, Folder 23, Letter, Bodwell to Ayres, December 19, 1933. In 1930, the Forest Society assumed management of all concessions within the notch when the state leased the former hotel concessions at Echo and Profile Lakes to the Forest Society, as well as the Lafayette Place Cabin following its construction.
392. UNH, Box 9, Folder 23, Letter, Bodwell to Ayres, December 19, 1933.
393. UNH, Box 10, Folder 10, Letter, Bodwell to Ayres, February 6, 1934.
394. UNH, Box 10, Folder 8, Letter, Bodwell to Ayres, February 17, 1934.
395. "Cold," *Vermont Telegraph* (Brandon), March 10, 1836, 3.
396. Miscellaneous Paragraphs," *Watertown (WI) Republican*, March 19, 1884, 7.
397. Starr King, *White Hills*, 125.
398. Samuel C. Eastman, *The White Mountain Guidebook*, 2nd ed. (Concord, NH: E.C. Eastman, 1859), 98.
399. Paul R. Jenks, "The Franconia Notch," *The Granite Monthly* 31, no. 2 (August 1901): 108.
400. W. Dustin White, "Snowshoeing in the White Mountains," *Forest and Stream* 82, no. 5 (January 31, 1914): 134.
401. Kenneth Dudley Smith, "Winter-Trips Among the White Mountains," *Photo-Era Magazine* 48, no. 2 (February 22): 72, 73.
402. Reverend H.J. Foote, "The Flume in Winter," *The Granite Monthly* 56, no. 4 (April 1924).

403. See Paul F. Hannah, "Franconia Notch in Winter," *The Granite Monthly* 60, no. 1 (January 1928): 64–67.
404. Smith, "Winter-Trips Among the White Mountains," 71.
405. See February 8, 1922 letter of Rufus M. Eastman, Littleton, NH, who after reading Smith's article in *Photo-Era* was anxious to make a similar trip ["One of Many," *Photo-Era Magazine* 48, no. 4 (April 1922): 232].
406. Although the Taft Trail began being cut in 1932, it was not until completion of the aerial tramway in 1938 that Cannon Mountain's popularity took off.
407. "Snow Train Crowd Breaks All Records," *BG*, February 5, 1934, 9.
408. "B. & M. Excursionists Enjoy New Hampshire Snowstorm," *BG*, March 9, 1931, 12.
409. "Snow Train Crowd Breaks All Records," *BG*, February 4, 1934, 9.
410. Bowles, *Let Me Show You New Hampshire*, 338.
411. "Bathhouse Is Proposed for Echo Lake," *NT*, September 11, 1941, 10.
412. UNH, Box 10, Folder 8, Letter, Ayres to Bodwell, November 24, 1934.
413. Ibid.
414. UNH, Box 10, Folder 10, Letter, Bodwell to Allen Hollis, September 22, 1938.
415. "Flume Reservation," *FN* 3, no. 2 (July 1939). The hurricane also provided the opportunity to provide firefighting training to "outdoor employees" of the Flume, as the debris constituted a potential fire hazard. A portable power pump and other firefighting apparatus were acquired, and the men were trained by state and federal officials in building fire lines and fighting forest fires.
416. Christopher Janus, "New England Ready," *NYT*, May 21, 1939, XX1; Eleanor Early, "Down East Carries On," *NYT*, October 9, 1938, 178.
417. "The Flume and Lost River Reservations," *FN* 9, no. 2 (May 1940): 20.
418. "Odd Items from Everywhere," *BG*, May 3, 1941, 10. At the time, salvaged timber was also employed in re-flooring the Flume Covered Bridge.
419. "Cabin Owners Protest Plan for Gasless Sunday," *NT*, June 12, 1941, 7.
420. "Tax Payers' Head Estimates N.H. Recreation 75 Per-cent," *DN*, September 18, 1942, 3.
421. "White Mountains Have an Appeal to Visitors," *BG*, June 14, 1942, E2.
422. Among the hotels not opening were the Mount Washington Hotel at Bretton Woods, Forest Hills Hotel at Franconia, Twin Mountain House at Carroll and the Maplewood at Bethlehem. The Maplewood used its grounds for food production.

423. "Ceremony of Transfer," *FN* 12, no. 1 (February 1948): 14. See also "The Flume Reservation," *FN* 9, no. 2 (June 1945).

Chapter 9

424. "Free Franconia Notch Is Sought," *MU*, December 4, 1934.
425. "Charge State Competition Hurst Recreation Business," *NT*, April 9, 1947, 5. See also Newell Brown, "News from the State Capitol," *Milford (NH) Cabinet*, April 17, 1947, 8.
426. Title was transferred on September 25, 1947. GD, Book 762, p. 463.
427. "Governor Takes Title to Remaining Notch Park Land," *NT*, October 3, 1947, 11.
428. "Ceremony of Transfer," *FN* 12, no. 1 (February 1948).
429. Shurcliff quoted in Frances Ann Johnson Hancock, *Saving the Great Stone Face: The Chronicle of the Old Man of the Mountain* (Canaan, NH: Phoenix Publishing, 1984), 85.
430. "Ceremony of Transfer," *FN* 12, no. 1 (February 1948). Brown was an executive of the Berlin, New Hampshire–based Brown Company, a paper and pulp manufacturing firm.
431. Ibid.
432. Curtiss, *Sloppy Dingle*, 268.
433. Rowena H. Morse, "New Hampshire Keeps Open House," *NYT*, June 6, 1948, XX7.
434. Advertisement, *NYT*, June 15, 1947, X17.
435. Mitchell Goodman, "Bus Tours in New England," *NYT*, June 7, 1959, XX31.
436. See G. Henry Crawford, "The Flume," *New Hampshire Profiles* 6, no. 7 (July 1957): 24–27, and *New Hampshire Profiles* 13, no. 6 (June 1964) for examples.
437. Mitchell Goodman, "Streamlining New Hampshire's Tour," *NYT*, June 22, 1958, XX16.
438. "Forest Preservation," *NYT*, July 10, 1938, 58.
439. *Waugh's Blue Book of Leading Hotels and Resorts of the World* (Boston: W. Wallace Waugh & Son, 1907), 72; Woodbury, *Littleton Courier*.
440. Bass, "Franconia Notch in Danger."
441 "Motor Tours to the White Mountains", *NYT*, August 7, 1926.
442. Hancock, *Saving the Great Stone Face*, provides an exceptional overview of the controversial I-93 proposal and planning process.

443. A.S. Plotkin, "Fight to Keep Franconia Notch Unsullied," *BG*, September 20, 1959, A78.
444. Volpe quoted in "Franconia Notch: Highway Battle Site," *NYT*, July 29, 1974, 25.
445. *United States Federal Highway Administration. Interstate Route 93—Franconia Notch and Alternate Routes: Draft Environmental Impact Statement*, 1979, B-19.
446. 1985 Commentator Edward DeCourcy in the *Argus-Champion* considered construction of the road in summer 1985 with its gravel, uncompleted bridges and overpasses: "As for me, what with all the construction work and piles of rock and gravel and partly completed bridges and overpasses, I felt somehow as though I had intruded on a lady changing her clothes" ["The Notch in Mid-Passage," *Argus Champion* (Newport, NH), August 14, 1985, 4].
447. *United States Federal Highway Administration. Interstate Route 93—Franconia Notch and Alternate Routes: Draft Environmental Impact Statement*, 1979, V-41.
448. "Nature Trail Opened," *DN*, September 16, 1971, 10.
449. *United States Federal Highway Administration. Interstate Route 93—Franconia Notch and Alternate Routes: Draft Environmental Impact Statement*, 1979, VII-15 and VII-16. The report estimated a facility carrying capacity of 7,200 for the Flume [p. V-42].
450. Ibid., VII-15 and VII-16.
451. Letter, George Gilman to John A. Clements, Commissioner, New Hampshire Department of Public Works and Highways, May 19, 1978, in *United States Federal Highway Administration. Interstate Route 93—Franconia Notch and Alternate Routes: Draft Environmental Impact Statement*, 1979, VIII-26 and VIII-27. Gilman argued that the majority of structures failed to meet the fifty-year cut-off period to be considered historic while the Souvenir Shop and barn had been too architecturally compromised because of later modification to be significant. The decision appears to have been made on the basis of a visual analysis of the structures combined with flawed data regarding the buildings' histories. See section V-31 of the impact statement, which gives inaccurate dates for several of the Flume structures. The decision overlooked the significance of the complex in documenting early twentieth-century development of roadside tourist attractions in the White Mountains.
452. Director of State Parks Paul Doherty, quoted in "State Park Has Record Season," *DN*, October 29, 1981, 30.
453. *Argus-Champion* quoted in "Gift Shops or Junk Shops?," *Milford (NH) Cabinet*, August 6, 1970, 11.

454. "Quotables," *The Messenger* (Hillsboro, NH), September 1, 1982, 5.
455. Trip Advisor, "Flume Gorge," www.tripadvisor.com/ShowUserReviews-g46088-d105518-r588318114-Flume_Gorge-Franconia_New_Hampshire.html (accessed June 14, 2018).
456. See New Hampshire Public Radio, "The Exchange," July 31, 2014, for a discussion of the then status of New Hampshire state parks and a consideration of the self-funding model.
457. See Jack Kenny, "Ten Years After: Region's Businesses Still Picking Up the Pieces a Decade after the Old Man of the Mountain Fell," *New Hampshire Business Review*, May 3, 2013. Kenny provides a consideration of the financial impact of the loss of the Old Man on the Flume and Cannon Mountain Aerial Tramway.
458. *State of New Hampshire, Department of Natural and Cultural Resources, Division of Parks and Recreation, Fiscal Year 2017 Financial Report.* Reflective of the turnaround were new logo designs that were introduced for nine of the state park system's most iconic sites, including the Flume, in 2011. Sold as patches and pins, the logos were also used for branding purposes.

Conclusion

459. Adams quoted in Enoch Shenton, "State House Journal," *PT*, October 16, 1947, 6.

INDEX

L

M

P

R

S

T

W

ABOUT THE AUTHOR

Historian Michael J. Maddigan has been engaged in research, writing and historic preservation for over thirty years. He is the author of several previous books on New England regional history. A native of Massachusetts, he is the founder of Recollecting Nemasket, a small publishing press devoted to the history of southeastern Massachusetts. A graduate of Stonehill College, he holds a master of arts degree from the Maxwell School of Citizenship and Public Affairs at Syracuse University. When not tramping about the White Mountains, he makes his home in a renovated 1863 woolen mill. To learn more about Mike's work, visit www.recollectingnemasket.com.